Whom Shall I Fear?

ೞ

A Strategy for Battling Fear and Anxiety
from Psalm 27

TONY SANELLI

Published by Christ Above All Publications
a ministry of
Grace Bible Church of Pleasant Hill, CA

These transcribed messages have been edited and formatted for
this publication. This is not a technical work, and as such,
footnotes and references to other material have been kept to a
minimum. Where a direct quote has been utilized all reasonable
attempts to locate the original source have been made

Cover Design by Dorothy Castel

ISBN: 1-948194-03-7
ISBN-13: 978-1-948194-03-7

"Here is clear medicine for anxiety-stricken hearts. In Whom Shall I Fear? Tony Sanelli unpacks the riches of Psalm 27 with pastoral sensitivity and Christ-centered application. Each chapter invites the reader to reflect upon a grace-given, Spirit-empowered capacity for battling unbelief. It is wise, insightful and will be an excellent resource for pastoral ministry as well."

Alexander Strauch,
Pastor and Author of "Biblical Eldership: An Urgent Call to Restore Biblical Church Leadership"

"I teach a preaching course at RTS in which I teach my students what I look for in a sermon. Each of these sermons does an excellent job. They faithfully expound the text. They make practical application to believers today. They tie the message of the text to the central biblical message of redemption. And they are grounded in sound theology. The sermons are very readable and relatable. The use of illustrations, quotations, and other biblical references is very effective. The purpose of helping the anxious is always in view and tied to the text. I am sure that many will benefit."

Dr James R. Newheiser,
Director of the Christian Counseling Program and Associate Professor of Christian Counseling & Pastoral Theology at Reformed Theological Seminary, Charlotte.

"The Psalms are like a mirror, often expressing the whole range of human emotions. In this book, Tony shepherds the reader through Psalm 27 in order to give hope and answers for the common emotions of fear and anxiety. He gives us wisdom on how to have faith in God in the midst of our troubles, and even when we don't understand what God is doing in our lives, how to wait upon his character. I highly recommend you read and meditate on this book."

Dr. Ryan Rippee
President and Professor of Church History & Theology at The Cornerstone Bible College and Seminary

DEDICATION

To my fellow elders of Grace Bible Church of Pleasant Hill, California. You lovingly and faithfully ministered to Christ's anxious flock during the distressing trials of 2020 by consistently pointing them to the One who alone is our light, salvation and stronghold. I remain forever grateful.

And the Lord's servant must not be quarrelsome but kind to everyone, able to teach, patiently enduring evil, correcting his opponents with gentleness.

2 Timothy 2:24-25a

CONTENTS

Psalm 27

	Introduction	1
1	Trusting	13
2	Seeking	33
3	Asking	57
4	Following	79
5	Waiting	99
	Epilogue	127

PSALM 27
OF DAVID

The Lord is my light and my salvation; whom shall I fear?
The Lord is the stronghold of my life; of whom shall I be afraid?
When evildoers assail me to eat up my flesh, my adversaries and
foes, it is they who stumble and fall.
Though an army encamp against me, my heart shall not fear;
though war arise against me, yet I will be confident.

One thing have I asked of the Lord, that will I seek after:
that I may dwell in the house of the Lord all the days of my life,
to gaze upon the beauty of the Lord and to inquire in his temple.
For he will hide me in his shelter in the day of trouble;
he will conceal me under the cover of his tent; he will lift me high
upon a rock.
And now my head shall be lifted up above my enemies all around
me, and I will offer in his tent sacrifices with shouts of joy;
I will sing and make melody to the Lord.

Hear, O Lord,
when I cry aloud; be gracious to me and answer me!
You have said, "Seek my face." My heart says to you, "Your face,
Lord, do I seek."
Hide not your face from me. Turn not your servant away in
anger, O you who have been my help.
Cast me not off; forsake me not, O God of my salvation!
For my father and my mother have forsaken me, but the Lord
will take me in.

Teach me your way, O Lord, and lead me on a level path because
of my enemies.
Give me not up to the will of my adversaries;
for false witnesses have risen against me,
and they breathe out violence.

I believe that I shall look upon the goodness of the Lord in the
land of the living!
Wait for the Lord; be strong, and let your heart take courage; wait
for the Lord!

INTRODUCTION

You've had a good life for the most part. Not a perfect life, but one that has often brought you some measure of joy and others even envied at times. But then the phone call came that rocked that once steady undercurrent of blessedness. It is now the first thing you think about when you awake. It is the first thing that leaps into your imagination when your mind is not otherwise occupied with simple tasks. You find yourself mumbling about it under your breath. Anxiety has become the new undercurrent of your life. It is the air you breathe. It is the white noise in the background. Sometimes it is almost the only thing you can think about. You are not alone in this. This became a reality for countless individuals soon after the spread of Covid-19 began in 2020. The hopes, plans and dreams of millions were shattered and anxiety reached a fever pitch as the pandemic spread like a tsunami across the globe. People who had never really considered themselves anxious types or worrisome became dominated by their fears.

This is a book for people who are prone to struggle with fear and anxiety and often find themselves unsure of what to do about it—how to respond from a biblical perspective. The struggle against anxiety for believers often increases the burden of guilt because most realize that Jesus and Paul command believers to *not* be anxious. Anxiety is therefore in the category of sin. This in itself is the source of much anxiety! In Matthew 6:25 our Lord clearly states, "Do not be anxious about your life." He then offers several reasons to not be anxious and finally firmly restates his exhortation in verse 34, "Therefore do not be anxious about tomorrow, for tomorrow will be anxious for itself." The apostle Paul also commands, "do not be anxious about anything" (Phil. 4:6), rather learn, as he has in Christ, "to be content" in whatever situation we might find ourselves (Phil. 4:11). It is clear that believers are commanded to battle against anxiety. It is also clear that the opposite of anxiety is a life of trusting faith and contentment in Christ. So why is this so elusive? Why is it that overcoming anxiety can be such a struggle?

I want to affirm at the very beginning that some anxiety can be the result of physiological problems. Some anxiety is born of hormonal imbalances and other health related problems. There is an interdependent continuum between our human physiology and spirituality—between body and soul. Drawing a clear line between the two is often not very simple nor absolutely clear. Physiological problems are not simply "healed," as it were, by spiritual growth. However, our *response* to all physical ailments is a spiritual matter and this study, I trust will be of benefit in those cases as well.

I also want to affirm that fears and anxieties are normal human experiences in a sin-broken world. David Powlison, Biblical counselor, author, and teacher, says, "Anxiety is a God-given capacity for knowing that something bad is going on in your world."[1] In other words, it's somewhat like a

---

[1] David Powlison, *Overcoming Anxiety,* New Growth Press, (Greensboro: CCEF, 2011), 4.

smoke alarm. It is a signal of present danger. When we become alert and then distressed over some evil we see and experience, we are acknowledging as God's creatures that this brokenness is not how it ought to be. We, like the rest of God's creation, eagerly wait for the day when sin will be no more (Rom. 8:19-21). We should be grateful that we have the capacity to care and the capacity to feel that something is wrong with our children, with our life, etc., for God has instilled this emotional response within us that, hearing the alarm, we may seek him and act in accordance with biblical wisdom. Powlison adds, "There's a right kind of anxiety that leads us to express loving concern for others in the midst of their trouble and draws us to take refuge in God when we are in trouble."[2]

Even the great apostle Paul openly admits that he experienced anxiety for all the churches (2 Corinthians 11:28). The truth is, until Jesus returns to gather his elect and abolish all causes of anxiety, we will all experience this anxious tension to some degree. It is right and proper. Thus, the goal is not to *never* fear or be anxious about anything at all (that would be impossible—a life with no alarms ever going off!), but to grow in our understanding of how to biblically respond to the anxiety-producing events we all experience in this broken creation. The goal is to not live *dominated* and *directed* by fears and anxieties that may or may not be rooted in matters that we can resolve. Rather, the goal is to so walk in the grace of God when facing anxiety that we can find peace and bring glory and honor to Christ. Some things we will never fix. But Christ can bring a steady peace to our hearts in the midst of them. The goal is less anxiety and more peace and stability in Christ.

---

[2] *Powlison*, 4.

Lastly, I want to also assure the reader that I write not only as a pastor but also as one who experiences the same turbulent waters of anxiety. When I began to compose this introduction long before the pandemic of 2020, I had been in the midst of a combination of situations that conspired to steal my joy for many months. They were indeed the first thing I thought about when I awoke. Like a dull pinched nerve in my soul, they throbbed constantly. One of them is a profound ache because it threatens those I love to this day, and I can do absolutely nothing about it. I often feel weak and powerless before it. Much anxiety rises out of a desire to reach out and control such problems. But I can't. It feels like a giant teetering stone that may roll down upon me at any unannounced moment. This is what led me to preach a series of sermons on Psalm 27 in which I found great spiritual help during this season of my life. These sermons became the basis of this book.

Perhaps you feel today somewhat like I did then. Some of you have problems unsolved; tensions unsettled or even existential threats. They may be financial or relational. They may have to do with your career, health, education or your family. You surely know what they are. You didn't plan for them, but they are in the fabric of your life now. You cannot control them. I want to encourage you yet again that the operating system that God has built into you is functioning as it should. The alarm is a signal of danger. Now, what to do about that alarm? How are we to faithfully engage in the battle against fear and anxiety?

~

If anyone had reason to fear or experience anxiety it was king David, the author of Psalm 27. We don't know exactly what his circumstances were, but his life was frequently at risk. When he uses words like "adversaries and foes," and "armies and wars," and "assail' and "eat up my flesh," these aren't exaggerations! He isn't simply waxing poetic. No, these were terrifyingly *real-life* situations that David *really* experienced, and the Bible is honest about his travails. For a time in his life, although he had been anointed king, David was chased and hunted down like an animal by King Saul, and he had to flee for his life. Temptation to fear and opportunity to dread his future were no doubt daily companions to David. Later in his reign as king of Israel, he was painfully betrayed by his own son, Absalom, who ran him out of his own kingdom, and David had to abandon his own town. Hurt, uncertainty, and distress filled his days once more. But as we read the psalms, we find that somehow, *amazingly*, David was able to see beyond his immediate circumstances and regain a heart at rest. That's one of the fascinating things about this man David; he was able to see *through* his circumstances, to his God beyond, and grasp onto some aspect of the character of God that gave him confidence and comfort. He was able to see *who* and *what* God was for him in the midst of his many difficulties. And this psalm, I believe, helps us all along that same road towards this same heart at rest. In writing and leaving it to us, David lays out for us a well-worn path to follow, giving us insight into how to battle and face our own anxieties.

So, pause for a moment and reflect before you continue to read. What is *your* greatest fear? What crisis perhaps lies before you, or that you fear may come upon you as you read this today? Is it your finances? For many of us, this is the case, and trusting the Lord with providing for all our material needs continues to be an up-and-down struggle throughout our lives. Perhaps that is you. Or maybe it has to do with your failing health, or the health of a loved one of yours, or your finances *because* of your health! In addition, for many of us, there is also a deeply embedded fear of failure in some facet of our life where we feel the need to perform, because we find our identity and security from succeeding in that area. Perhaps for some of us it's the possibility of failing at school or failing in some business venture that we're embarking on, or even more painfully, failing at relationships. And a few of us may fear for our children's future and their path of life as it unfolds before our eyes. Perhaps it's the fear of loneliness, and we're thinking, "I'll be like this forever."

Whatever it may be, before we begin our study in this psalm, I believe it is essential to understand that underneath all of these examples lies a deeper struggle, and that is this: wrestling with the temptation to find our security and self-image in something or someone other than God. Many of our anxieties are rooted in the feeling that what we value most is about to be taken away, and when it is threatened, our very identity will collapse, and we react with fear and panic. This reveals to us that our heart has shifted from seeing God alone as the source of our true and lasting peace and joy to desiring something else. There's an idolatry of the heart harboring in our souls. In other words, when our "little g" god is being threatened, we feel troubled because we've not had our eyes on the "big G" God in our lives. Consider what Timothy Keller says, "My fears are directly proportional to the vulnerability of the things that are my greatest joys. If the thing that is my greatest joy is God, I will live without fear. If my one thing ... the thing I most want ... is God, I am safe."[3] Even more simply, Powlison writes, "All the things we worry about are what we want but could lose.

---

[3] Timothy J. Keller, *The Timothy Keller Sermon Archive* (New York City: Redeemer Presbyterian Church), 2013.

That's why we worry. The best thing you could ever want you will never lose."[4]

I am convinced that David was a believer who found comfort and solace in the midst of his trials because he had his eyes and heart firmly set on the God of all gods, the one who anchored his soul in stability and peace when everything else in his life appeared to be slipping away. He was David's greatest joy and what he wanted most. Psalm 27 will help us see how he achieved this and follow the same path. I believe this psalm can be of great help for all of you, as it has been for me. It is especially helpful when we, as New Covenant believers in Jesus, see the psalm through the lens of Christ and the gospel, and that is our aim in this book as we study Psalm 27 together, a psalm rich and beautiful in its multifaceted expression of faith in the midst of fears.

A High Perch View of Psalm 27

Before we launch into the details of our study, let's take a moment to put on our binoculars and glass over the historical and literary context of Psalm 27 and how it's put together. The book of Psalms is, as one of my mentors was fond to say, an Old Testament "poetic pointer to King Jesus." While each psalm is a self-contained poem, David and later authors have arranged these poems in a certain order to create and maintain a narrative trajectory. Book 1 (Psalms 1-41) is primarily concerned with telling the story of David and his rise to power. His rise was one marked by betrayal and suffering. Yet this was but a faint picture of the similar arduous path for the greater David to come. Our Lord Jesus

---

[4] David Powlison, *Worry – Pursuing a Better Path to Peace* (Phillipsburg: P&R Publishing, 2004), 26.

faced threats from our arch enemy, was surrounded by false witnesses who breathed out violence and knew the deepest betrayal as God's true king. He knows better than anyone the pressures that have the power to produce great anxiety in our lives.

While the specific historical setting of Psalm 27 is not clear, the lack of detailed historical information does not obscure the clarity of the main theme. I believe Psalm 27 is *a poetic expression of David's absolute confidence in God that leads him to seek the Lord above all else.* This confidence lies not in David's own abilities or strengths but in the Lord. Though the psalm clearly includes lamentation, it rises above lamentation and builds upon the final statement of hope from Psalm 26—"My foot stands on level ground; in the great assembly I will bless the Lord." It is on this "level ground" that David articulates his resolute confidence in Psalm 27. David remains confident throughout and concludes the psalm with a call for others to share his confidence and wait upon the Lord. His confidence and singular motivation point to the life and devotion of Jesus Christ whose confidence in the Father led Him to "set his face to go to Jerusalem" (Luke 9:51) despite the promise of severe opposition and suffering that awaited Him. In Hebrews, we learn that he did this all for the "joy that lay before him" (Heb. 12:2).

The psalm itself and its structure has two major sections: verses 1-6, and verses 7-14. On the surface they appear almost as polar opposites. The first half, verses 1-6, exudes a certain confidence: "Though an army encamp against me, my heart shall not fear; though war arise against me, yet I will be confident." Nothing is going to stop this man from conquering and emerging victorious! But then, in verses 7-14, there's the sense of a desperate plea: "Hear, O LORD, when I cry aloud; be gracious to me and answer me!" Now this sounds like the prayer of a man in desperation. These conflicting tones has led some biblical commentators to suggest that these are in fact two separate psalms that somebody crudely stuck together. But on the contrary, do we not all know what fallen human life is like in that our hearts and emotions can quickly vacillate from one extreme to the other? We all know this from our own shifting emotions.

Furthermore, as Allen Ross notes,[5] there are also many verbal connections between both halves of this psalm, and when stepping back, one can see that the whole psalm is bracketed with a uniting sense of confidence. It begins that way, and verse 13 affirms assuredly, as well, "I believe that I shall look upon the goodness of the LORD in the land of the living!" Thus, I conclude this is one psalm written by one man reflecting on how he was facing the fears and the challenges in his life through his relationship with the Lord. Cannot you recall a time when courage failed you, yet in the next moment you felt yourself being built up in faith by the Spirit to pray, only to sink once more into fear and despair? This psalm reveals the heart of one man who has. And then there is the very last verse: "Wait for the LORD; be strong, and let your heart take courage; wait for the LORD!" That concluding exhortation to wait for the Lord calls us to once again rise up with David and with our eyes on the greater David, Jesus, by God's grace, live the same life of faith that he expresses in this psalm.

---

[5] Allen P. Ross, *A Commentary on the Psalms*: Vol. 1, Kregel Exegetical Library, (Grand Rapids: Kregel Publications, 2011), 624.

A Strategy of Faith for Facing Fears and Anxiety

As we have seen, David had good reasons to be afraid, as
many of you do, too. And I propose that Psalm 27 offers a
strategy for believers to battle and overcome fear and anxiety.
I see five anxiety-conquering components within this
strategy of faith that will empower us to face them.[6] This is
not to imply that we have to work through each of these in
the same strict sequence nor that one is more important than
the others per se. There may be days or seasons where God
leads you to concentrate on a few specific ones, or within a
day or week you may meditate upon all of them. I pray that
whatever fears and anxieties you are facing, you will find that
going back and practicing one or all of these will help you to
see beyond your circumstances, lay hold of God in Christ by
faith and secure a heart of courage and strength in the midst
of your battle. Here I've provided a chart of all five of them,
and we will make our way steadily through each of them one
chapter at a time.

---

[6] I am indebted to Timothy Keller for the notion of a strategy being revealed in
Psalm 27, though his organization of the psalm is very different from mine.
This came largely from a sermon on this psalm found in *The Timothy Keller
Sermon Archive* (New York City: Redeemer Presbyterian Church, 2013).

Trusting	Verses 1-3	*The Lord is my light, my salvation, my stronghold. I will be confident.*
Seeking	Verses 4-6	*One thing I have asked of the Lord, that will I seek after: that I might dwell in the house of the Lord all the days of my life.*
Asking	Verses 7-10	*Hear Oh lord, when I cry aloud, be gracious to me and answer me.*
Following	Verses 11-12	*Teach me your way, O Lord, and lead me on a level path.*
Waiting	Verses 13-14	*I believe that I shall look upon the goodness of the Lord in the land of the living! Wait for the Lord.*

Whom Shall I Fear?

1

TRUSTING

The LORD is my light and my salvation; whom shall I fear?
The LORD is the stronghold of my life; of whom shall I be afraid?
Psalm 27:1

The psalm begins with a strong assertion of confidence
in Yahweh,[7] the LORD. It is essentially a confession of faith.
The Lord is affirmed to be David's *light*, *salvation* and
stronghold. These three terms together suggest that David is
focusing on God's protective role in his life, on God as his
shield. In many other passages of the Bible, especially the
psalms, God's protection is described with similar rich
imagery. Words like *strong tower*, *refuge*, *fortress*, *mighty rock*, *shelter
of the Most High*, and *rampart* all describe God's protective
shielding power and love for those who fear him. We must
acknowledge the three terms that David uses each imply a

---

[7] This name is the covenant name of God revealed to Moses at the burning bush
in Exodus 3. It is almost always translated LORD (all caps) in the English
Bible. The Hebrew would be pronounced something like "Yahweh."

certain amount of danger present in his life. The reader gets the sense that David is drawing upon past history. He has experienced first-hand God's protective presence in his life as his light, salvation and stronghold.

Light implies that there is darkness in David's life. *Salvation* implies that there are threats in David's life that he needs saving from. And *stronghold* implies that there are enemy attacks from which he seeks a place of refuge. This psalm was not written solely against oppositions primarily of the spiritual type, but from a place of physical danger and at a time of great need.

So what gives David the courage in the midst of these perils to boldly ask the rhetorical question "whom shall I fear? Of whom shall I be afraid?" (the answer is no one!) Verse 2 provides the answer for these questions in verse 1. It is because when evil doers assail him to eat up his flesh, his adversaries and foes, it is they who stumble and fall. In other words, this literal faltering of his enemies in the midst of their persecution of him is where the courage of verse 1 comes from. He has witnessed their floundering and can see God's favor and preservation of his life, both body and soul, as did our Lord Jesus when he was surrounded by those vehemently seeking his crucifixion. We can attest that to David this is a real means of assurance and confidence—to have seen God work in such a direct way in his life! This can be a life-long means of encouragement to us today as well, when our memory continually bears witness to the Lord's direct intervention in our lives for our good and our defense.

I want to stress that while the Hebrew verb here for "assail" is translated in the present tense, it can be, and probably ought to be, translated as a past tense, "when evildoers *assailed* me... it is they who stumbled and fell." Consequently, this is a bit of an autobiography. In other words, David can say what he says in verse 1 because he *has seen* God protect him many times and he now writes about this in verse 2. God has been the pinnacle of light, salvation and stronghold for all of his days. Insightfully, Alexander Maclaren points out that the language employed in verse 2 has a remarkable correspondence with that used in the earlier story of David's fight with the giant Goliath.[8] There we find a correspondence between the verbs *assail* and *fall* used repeatedly in the famous battle story with Goliath that are used here as well. Maybe that's what David had in his mind. He's seen giants fall; he has experienced God's protection. He has seen even greater enemies not only stumble but completely crumble by the hand of God, and that's what gives him confidence. It was a Puritan, Richard Sibbes, who reflecting upon this psalm said, "Experience breeds hope and confidence."[9] When you go through difficult things in life, note them and remember them. Remember what God did before, because he's consistent. He's the same yesterday, today and forever.

I remember a time years ago when my family and I were on a trip in Costa Rica, driving far and deep into the tropical countryside. We'd come to one of those Central American bridges (the kind that would under most circumstances have CAUTION yellow tape around them here in the U.S.!). We looked at the bridge and pulled over. We sat there, peering out the windows of the car, uncertainty etched on our tourist faces. We were each silently judging whether or not we could safely drive across it. From everything we saw, it looked doubtful. The flimsy, creaking bridge had ancient, rotted wood planks, and the rusty iron framework whistled in the wind. It appeared to the uninitiated traveler to be "dangling by a thread", as it were. It was held up by a pair of cracked posts on either side of the jungle gorge and leafy vines that

---

[8]Alexander Maclaren, *The Psalms,* Vol. 1, (Minneapolis: Klock & Klock, reprinted 1981), 261.
[9] Richard Sibbes, *A Breathing after God,* (USA: Pavlik Press, reprinted 2012), 116, Kindle.

had become twisted and woven into the side railings and along the top. And while we were sitting there thinking, and probably each quietly praying to ourselves, a small busload of locals just sped right by us shouting, "Hola!" and zoomed right across it!

Why did they go across so dauntlessly? Because they would go across that bridge many times every day, a small bus full of them! Difficult to imagine but true. Indeed, "experience breeds hope and confidence." We had no experience with that bridge or any other like it, and so we came to a bumpy halt. But if you have been a Christian for some time, you have had a lot of experience already! So, if you would but ask God to help you, and remember what he's already done and been for you, you will find your courage rising. Recall specifically a time in your life when God led you by the hand across your own swaying bridge and safely onto the other side. When the future's frightening uncertainty flashes across your mind, or the details of a difficult situation threaten to loop over and over in your pacing thoughts, polish your trophies, as they say, of God's past faithfulness to you, and steady your heart.

Reject those worries that doubt the Lord's loving care over you, and instead pull out past remembrances of his provision for you. Perhaps that might look like maintaining a written or digital journal of his answer to your prayers about something personal like when he provided you with something you didn't even know you needed, or hadn't told anyone about, but he knew. And he provided it for you. Pray to him, conversing with him about all the ways he has met your needs and calmed your fears in the past, and praise him for his goodness, kindness, compassion and strength. Remember what he's been to you.

David's reflection in verse 2 of his enemies' slipping now gives rise in verse 3 to his present trust and confidence as he thinks of the future: "Though an army encamp against me, my heart shall not fear; though war arise against me, yet I will be confident." David is faithfully rehearsing the past and trusting God's protection in light of his past experiences of God's sheltering love. The ESV and NIV translation of the verb in the phrase, "I will be confident," actually obscures the more typical translation of, "I will *trust.*" This second translation corresponds contextually with neighboring psalms that have similar themes. For example, Psalm 25:2 says, "O my God, in you I trust." In Psalm 26:1, "I have trusted in the Lord without wavering," it is the same verb used for "trusted" as is used here at the end of Psalm 27:3 for "be confident." He also uses a form of the Hebrew participle which emphasizes that this is an immediate and continuing trust, not just for one moment. So in essence David is fearlessly saying, "Even though war rises against me, because of my past with God, I am trusting."

So we see that the first strategy of faith in overcoming our fears is *trusting.* At its core, the battle with anxiety is a struggle against unbelief—a struggle against doubt. It is a struggle for faith in God's Fatherly protection and faithfulness. We may then sum up the central doctrine of these first three verses as: ***faith begins to overcome fear and anxiety by trusting in God's protective love as experienced in the past.***

This protective love is described as the three images of light, salvation and stronghold. This is what David has known God to be for him all of his life as he reflects backward on a rescuing Savior. This is what he battles to believe again and again about his God. Let us now reflect on each of these images briefly though each of them is worthy of a chapter in itself.

Light

Light stands for many things in the Bible, including joy, knowledge, purity, and goodness.[10] But here in this context, the imagery being used is that of the Lord as the light that dispels the darkness of fear and anxiety. And darkness represents many things in the Scriptures as well, such as evil, confusion, gloom, and uncertainty, especially in the context of warfare or battle, which is what David is most likely reflecting upon. For him, the darkness can represent real death, and an overwhelming dread of the peril of death. It's been said of soldiers that they suffer a thousand deaths in reflecting upon just the one they may actually face. And I think that foreboding anticipation is probably what David experienced often in his life and that's what he's speaking about now. A group of several of the psalms starting from Psalm 23 are connected by this theme, and our Psalm 27 is reminiscent of Psalm 23:4 where he says that "even though I walk through the valley of the shadow of death, I will fear no evil, for you are with me." There's a correspondence between the dark valley of death and fear that is woven through many of David's psalms, Psalm 27 included.

Scientifically, total darkness is the absence of light. In other words, where light shines, darkness vanishes. They cannot coexist. When we go out camping, away from the bright city lights into the woods where no street lamps have been installed, we always bring flashlights, to shine a glow upon the camping spot and our tents. When the power goes out at a family dinner at home or when we explore deep caves, we use flashlights then too. We use them to illuminate the darkness, to remove it, revealing what was previously hidden and unknown. David says that is what God is to him. He is the light that dispels the darkness of fear. And notice two further things about this statement. He says, God *is* my

---

[10] See the excellent entry "Light" in the New Dictionary of Biblical Theology.

light. This is the only verse in the Old Testament that declares God *is* light. In other places, God gives light or God sheds light, God brings light or God creates light. But here David proclaims God *is* light. Of course, the New Testament says in various places, like in the books of John and 1 John, that "God is light and in Him there is no darkness at all." But in the Old Testament David alone refers directly to God as light. Then notice secondly the personal ownership that David claims about God: "The Lord (Yahweh) is *my* light." David is reflecting on his personal, individual communion with God. With these two declarations his emphasis is upon his relational fellowship with God. He is not speaking about the gifts *of* God, but about *God himself* when he proclaims that God is his light. In the depth of his communion with God, as David knows him, understands him, and meditates upon him, God is light to him. Knowing God is an illuminating and anxiety-conquering experience. How is this so?

Often our soul's distress surges out from the unknown, from that which is not illuminated. They rise up from the unseen and from what is potentially threatening to our lives. What if **this** happens? And what if **that** happens? What if this *and* that happens? We create pictures of a future that doesn't exist yet, which we don't know *will* exist, but yet we fear it. And fear thrives on the darkness of our worst imaginings and fretful projections. The more we imagine and think about the dangers, the more enveloped and filled with it we become, and it clouds all happiness and joy in our lives.

Let me tell you another story from our travels in Costa Rica. One time my wife Sheri and I were there visiting missionaries, and we borrowed their vehicle. Often vehicles belonging to missionaries in the field aren't the most trustworthy, and this proved the same for ours, so the missionary taught me five or six tricks on how to keep it moving. We had one night and the following morning to spend in enjoyment for recreation, so we drove deep through the back woods that late evening in that old, four-wheel drive jalopy, making our way across the backside of Arenal, one of Costa Rica's active and "youngest" volcanoes. There were no lights out there at all; no streetlights to soften the night. As we were making a long pass around the steeply sloping curves of the conical, lava-rocked mountain, I slowed down and, being the tease that I am, said, "Look how dark it is, Sheri," and then I clicked off the lights! I began slowly driving forward just a few feet at a time in the total pitch-dark. We couldn't see anything! We couldn't even see one flitting shape or shadow passing outside our windows or looming in the windshield. Just a deep, thick, black curtain. Unmercifully, I rolled down the windows saying, "Listen to the sounds of the jungle." At this point, the untrustworthiness of this old vehicle combined with the absolute darkness, the creepy insect and animal sounds of the jungle (not to mention an active volcano towering over us) became too much for my poor wife. After going along for twenty or thirty seconds, she panicked and cried out, "Turn them on! Turn them on!" Click! Back to safety and light (and an apology from me as well). We were still just on the road, of course, but when we couldn't see what was in front of us, Sheri's mind began to worry.

Our fears often resemble this experience on our dark road. They exist because we center our sense of security and well-being on knowing and seeing what is around us and in our lives. We like to see what's coming ahead. We feel a sense of control and knowledge that comforts us. When we think we know how the next few days or months should expect to go, we feel a safety net spread and fasten tight in our souls. It feels much easier to live by sight and not by faith. But when something that we depended on for our happiness begins to break, or disappear from our horizon, like being alone in the dark, we begin to fear our fate. Our health which once felt solid now becomes weak with disease. Our financial security is wiped away in one instant of disaster or poor investing. A family member walks away from the faith and their relationship with you. The truth is, so much of the future *is* utterly unknown to us; tomorrow is obscure to you and me. Like a veil which hangs dark and heavy in front of our path, the future is completely hidden from our knowledge. We may make plans, but we don't really know what is going to happen. But we DO know the one who possesses complete and faultless knowledge of tomorrow.

There is only one who knows what each new day brings and who can illumine your darkness, deepening your courage and faith. God knows every day of your life in the coming years, and every situation you'll face. Darkness can give rise to concern. Fears thrive in the dark and often so much of our anxiety is only of what is *potential* and not yet real. Charles H. Spurgeon once said, "The shadow of anticipated trouble to the timorous mind is a more prolific source of sorrow than the trouble itself."[11] We worry and fear situations from a tomorrow that doesn't exist yet.

To know God as our light does not imply that he *reveals* all the details of our individual futures, but rather he assures us that he does know what lies ahead and as our shepherd will not be caught off guard. To know the Lord as our light is to live with the understanding that our God has a sovereign plan for our lives, and he is in control of this plan moment by moment as we live out our days. It is to know that the future is HIS future. As David declares in Psalm 139:11-12, "If I say, 'Surely the darkness shall cover me, and the light about me be night,' even the darkness is not dark to you; the night is as bright as the day, for darkness is as light with you." And why is this so? Because, he goes on to say, "... in your book were written, every one of them, the days that were formed for me, when as yet there was none of them" (Psalm

---

[11] Charles H. Spurgeon, *The Treasury of David,* Vol. 1, (Nashville: Thomas Nelson Publishers, Reprinted 1984), 2.

139:16). What is dark about tomorrow to us is absolutely clear to our Lord who takes us by his hand and leads us onward.

To know God as our light is also to know things for what they truly are. What we imagine is often not the reality of what is being presented to us in our lives. My sister once told me a funny story about her and her husband. One day she came up to me and said, "You won't believe what happened last night!" I asked, "What happened??" She said, "All this commotion happened in the middle of the night!" She then told me that she must have made a sound while she was sleeping that startled her husband enough for him to wobbly stand up on the bed, still half-asleep. Then, grunting like a determined fighter, he dived across the room and started wrestling with something in the dark. All sorts of stuff began slamming around the room, noisily breaking! Now startled herself, my sister swiftly turned on the light and saw that he was wrestling the floor lamp! She stared at him for a few moments and then asked incredulously, "What are you doing?!" He paused, now fully awake. Gazing at the lamp, he began to laugh. He said, "I thought for sure you'd said there was someone in here, and I got up on the edge of the bed and I saw him. So I took him down!" When my sister finished telling me this crazy story, I could relate immediately because I remember being a young boy and often seeing things in the corners of my own childhood bedroom. Every time I was sure there was something in the corner, I would turn on the light to see...and discover it was just my coat.

God is the one who can "turn on the light" for us in our lives. The light of God's truth shows our fears for what they truly are. And we need his light to see and respond clearly to what he reveals to us. Remember what I said about soldiers dying a thousand deaths in fear of the one, in anticipation of the one? David too, was a soldier, as are all of us who fight the good fight of faith. So David, when faced with the fears that his mind anticipated, for the day, for the next week, for the next moment, he proclaimed truthfully to himself and to us that God is his light, and that through his nearness to David, God would dispel the darkness and shows things to be what they are. "In your light do we see light" (Psalm 36:9).

When we entrust our bodies, minds, and hearts daily to the God who alone sees all things, we unite our souls by faith to him, and we walk in his light. And his light becomes our light especially through his revelation to us—God's communication to us through his Word. God's Word reveals God's thoughts. God's Word is God speaking. And understanding all who he is and what he has done and will continue to do for us and for his glory through his Word is what dispels the darkness of the unknown and diminishes that which looks so threatening. David would write in Psalm 119:105, "Your word is a lamp to my feet and a light to my path."

As Christians today we know that God's light, His revelation, is supremely so to us in Jesus Christ, who is God's Word that became flesh. The New Testament tells us Jesus is the light of the world. John 1:5 says that He is, "the light that came into the world and the darkness could not overcome it…" because light pierces darkness. He is the light that obliterates the darkness of spiritual blindness and unbelief. He is the light that banishes the fear of judgment. How? Because our sins have been judged in Him already! We have no reason to fear wrath and banishment from God. He is the light that drives away utterly from our hearts the fearful darkness of what lies beyond the grave. Why is this true? Because he rose from the grave and his resurrection is the assurance of our own someday. So, as we know Jesus, as we walk with Jesus, as David walked with the Lord Yahweh, we are in His light and he overcomes the darkness. What Yahweh was to David, Christ is to you and me by 10-fold, we might say, for we have greater revelation in Him. David saw through the light of God's revelatory word that his Messiah was coming. Jesus fulfills this promise for David and every Christian today, as the apostle notes in John 8:12: "I am the light of the world; whoever follows me will not walk in darkness but will have the light of life." Spiritual life. Eternal life.

Christ, dear reader, is the light in your life that supremely removes fear. In the light of Christ, we see our problems and our trials for what they really are. They are not that which is going to ruin and destroy us. Instead we see trials and tribulations to be the productive tools of God himself. In the light of Christ, we see and understand that God "causes all things to work together for good for those who love God, for those who are called according to his purpose" (Romans 8:28-29). For we live with the assuring truth that God has loved us and has redeemed us through his Son, so every detail and event of our lives is for our future good and his ultimate glory. And in the light of Christ, we understand that trials, as James 1 tells us, can be received with joy because they will result in endurance, and endurance will produce perfection, a maturing into Christ-likeness fully whole and complete. In the light of Christ, we learn from Paul in 2 Corinthians 4:17-18, that whatever sufferings we face in this life will not ruin us or destroy us, but they are rather "light and momentary", and will soon fade away forever. They are also "preparing for us a weight of glory" that cannot even be compared to anything we can experience here on earth, difficult or pleasant. We begin to see that what we fear is only a lamp. It's only my coat. It's really and truly there, but it's not what we thought it was. It won't be your ruin, dear saint, but rather your victory. He will see you through this life, and whatever you face now or in the future, let me say this to you: if you are in Christ, it will not be to your ruin. It will be to your benefit.

"In the light of Christ," one commentator said, "inflated anxieties are reduced to reality."[12] I wholeheartedly concur. Though your health issues, your financial issues, your concerns about your children, your plans, your fears of failure are all real, they are inflated until you see them through the light of Christ. Let Christ be the light through which you see reality and find his peace.

Salvation

After naming God as his light, David next proclaims, "The Lord is my salvation." The word means *deliverance*. And again, it is the language of literal warfare in David's life at the time. *Deliverance* is a term that was used to emphasize God's capability to give David military victory, and to save him in battle, even when the odds were against him. God was always his salvation. We see in Scripture that God made many promises to David the King of Israel, who was the foreshadower of the Great King, and David was fully relying upon these promises of God. He knew his place, so to speak, to a degree, in redemptive history, just like Abraham who trusted God's promise to him earlier in the Scripture narrative. David, in like manner, says, "I will be delivered. God has said so. I still have to fight the battle, but at the end of the day I know that when I'm delivered it will be because of God. He'll be my deliverance." And God did deliver David and his people as well, often just when it seemed all hope was gone. Sometimes he would deliver them through human instruments, like when he raised up warrior judges such as Gideon. Sometimes it would be through direct intervention, like in the parting of the Red Sea. Deliverance by the hand of God, either directly or indirectly through human instruments, always proves God as the deliverer.

---

[12] Gerald H. Wilson, *Psalms*, vol. 1, The NIV Application Commentary (Grand Rapids: Zondervan, 2002), 490.

David didn't know how God specifically would save him, but he knew that whether God used the sword in his hand or a lightning bolt from the sky to slay his enemies, God would be his victory. David was so sure of God's saving power and rescue that he could approach the morning of battle dressage whispering, "I place no confidence in my human plans, but I cast myself wholly on the deliverance that will come from God." Now, this is not to say that we should not make any preparations for our future. Depending on God's deliverance does not mean to just sit idly by and wait, doing nothing. We need to plan and fight our battles as David did, but with a heart like his too, fully trusting that our salvation, when it comes, will be from the Lord.

Though spiritual deliverance is not primary in David's mind when he writes Psalm 27, in Christ we can understand this: ***Christians will find and have found deliverance from evil and from our greatest enemies, sin and death through God's salvation in Christ***. And many times these are the very sources of fear in people's lives. But because Jesus has taken our penalty on the cross, we believers have found redemption from our sins and guilt. Romans 8:1 tells us, "There is therefore now no condemnation for those who are in Christ Jesus." He has already been our liberation, spiritually speaking, from this greatest crisis, which is facing the horrors and terrors of God's condemnation and hell. There is no condemnation for those who are in Christ Jesus. Let that ring in your heart as you start up each new day. Pile up the sins of the past day, week, month, year and know this: there is still no condemnation for you, because he was condemned on your behalf. The Lord is our salvation, so, we absolutely can live free of that kind of fear rising up and dominating our hearts! The apostle John wrote similarly in 1 John 4:16-18:

So we have come to know and to believe the love that God has for us. God is love and whoever abides in love abides in God, and God abides in him. By this is love perfected with us so that we may have confidence for the day of judgment, because as he is so also are we in this world. There is no fear in love, but perfect love casts out fear. For fear has to do with punishment, and whoever fears has not been perfected in love. We love because he first loved us.

What John has in mind when he talks about perfected love is this: God's love for us brought to its perfected fullness in our lives, a love that only God can produce and bestow upon us. And this love is evidently abiding in us (placed there by God and from God), when we love one another. That's the love that comes from the Holy Spirit. And when we walk in this love, and experience this love, and are sharing this love with others, we are confident for the coming Day of Judgment. When somebody asks you, "Why are you loving like that?" You can reply, "Because he first loved me." And when someone asks, "How can you be so unafraid of this life, and of death?" You can resolutely respond, "Because he loves me now and always."

As we walk in and meditate on His love, we will grow ever surer that he has been our salvation, and we will fear no condemnation, no judgment. Fear has to do with judgment, but perfect love—that love produced in our lives by union with Christ through the Holy Spirit—casts out fear and reminds us that we are safe in him. In Christ, we've experienced deliverance from sin, not only its guilt but also, dear saint, its power—its control over our lives. The apostle Paul says in Romans 6:6, that if you are in Christ, you are no longer a slave to sin: "our old self was crucified with him...so that we would no longer be enslaved to sin." Though we will sin tomorrow, just like we did yesterday, we are no longer enslaved to it. We can walk in the joy of his saving love, because we have God's love and Christ's Spirit in us. He has been and will always be our salvation.

Stronghold

David lastly says that the Lord is his *stronghold*, a word that may mean *refuge*, or *a place of safety*. Picture standing at the base of the tallest mountain, its snow-dusted, craggy, jutting top so high and distant that it is hidden by clouds from your view. The base is miles wide, solidly thick, with sheer steep sides made of the densest rock on earth. It's a place that's impregnable. David says, *the Lord is my refuge*. He's that place of impregnable protection. He's the shield of his life. Think of heavily fortified places like Fort Knox, or NORAD (North American Aerospace Defense Command) in the Cheyenne mountains of Colorado. NORAD sits inside a hollowed-out space, and way down inside it has 25-ton blast doors surrounded by 1700 feet of granite (and that's just describing the physical elements of security that are there!) It's an unassailable bulwark. But Christ is a greater refuge still!

Proverbs 18:10 says, "The name of the Lord is a strong tower; the righteous man runs into it and is safe." When we run into the Lord, our strong tower, we resist the devil. He flees before the mountain and fortress of the Lord. When we fear the Lord, we fear no one else. And this is how David thought, believed, and lived. He says that the Lord had become his stronghold. Let's reflect on the spiritual implications of this image in Christ for you and me. Jesus is our spiritual refuge as well as our circumstantial and material refuge because all things lie in his hand. We often come to him with minds weary and burdened with much suffering. He is our spiritual refuge from emotional pain and through the physical difficulties of life. The wounds we carry in our hearts and on our bodies, he shoulders for us, for he is our stronghold. It is our greatest comfort to know that through our communion with him, we at all times have a friend in heaven who takes us into his sanctuary where we find nourishment and fresh strength through his care. Don't you enjoy having friends in high places?

A few years ago, my wife and I were trying to connect a phone landline to a remote property, and for some weeks we couldn't get AT&T's customer service to call us back and start the process. It was frustrating. I finally asked one of our friends, a church member who works for AT&T, for his help. Lo and behold, the next day I received a call from AT&T. It's nice to have friends in high places! The book of Hebrews describes our truest friend who advocates for us from on high. Hebrews 4 states that we have a friend at the right hand of the throne of heaven and he's our great high priest (Heb. 4:15-16). His presence there is his plea for God's love towards you to remain consistent. And it does! His love never wavers. We have a friend in heaven who empathizes, who will never say to you and me, "I can't relate to that." Whatever is on our hearts to share with him, he will listen and understand. He empathizes and he sustains us in our sufferings. Christ is our refuge, our stronghold. This does not mean that we will never suffer. But through our sufferings, we will be strengthened and held through to the end. That's the imagery of God as our fortress and ally, the most powerful, capable ally we have. David fought battles his whole life. But God was always his stronghold.

Notice how the Apostle Paul also reflects on how God is a comforting refuge for him in 2 Corinthians 1:3-5:

> *Blessed be the God and Father of our Lord Jesus Christ, the Father of mercies and God of all comfort, who comforts us in all our affliction, so that we may be able to comfort those who are in any affliction, with the comfort with which we ourselves are comforted by God. For as we share abundantly in Christ's sufferings, so through Christ we share abundantly in comfort too.*

In Paul's sufferings, Christ was always a stronghold to him, because Paul was never defeated by them. He was never destroyed by them, and suffering could never take away from him that which Christ gave him. No matter what! In the following verses Paul goes on to share that he was delivered from that specific event in his life, and he trusts that God would still be there to deliver him in the future. Again, it's not that believers never experience hardship. God may or may not keep us from distress, but it surely is this--God is our stronghold *through* our sufferings and as long as we belong to Christ, nothing of true and eternal value can ever be taken from us. Finances may swirl down the drain or our health may crumble. Truly we witnessed this on a global scale during the pandemic of 2020. We or someone we love may endure great pain, and though these things are real events creating real burdens, nothing you possess in Christ will ever be snatched from you. Reflect upon these words from Romans 8:35-39:

> *Who shall separate us from the love of Christ? Shall tribulation, or distress, or persecution, or famine, or nakedness, or danger, or sword? As it is written, 'For your sake, we are being killed all the day long; we are regarded as sheep to be slaughtered.' No, in all these things we are more than conquerors through him who loved us. For I am sure that neither death nor life, nor angels nor rulers, nor things present nor things to come, nor powers, nor height nor depth, nor anything else in all creation, shall be able to separate us from the love of God in Christ Jesus our Lord.*

Though we experience trouble in this life, he remains our steadfast God.

John Chrysostom was one of the early church fathers who faced persecution from the Empress Eudoxia and the Emperor Arcadius in the Byzantine Empire in the first century. The story has been recorded in various ways, quoted by many, and their complete accuracy only God knows. But Chrysostom is reported to have handled himself in this manner before Eudoxia: The Empress threatened Chrysostom with banishment if he remained a Christian, and he replied, "You can't banish me, for this world is my Father's house." "But I will slay you," said the Empress. And he said, "No, you can't, because my life is hidden with Christ in God." The Empress said, "I will take away your treasury." He answered, "No, you can't. My treasures are in heaven and my heart is there." And she said, "Well, I'll drive you from man so you'll have no friend left." Chrysostom said, "You can't do that either. I have a friend in heaven from whom you cannot separate me. I defy you. There is nothing you can do to hurt me." This story, whether completely true or not, certainly reflects the confidence Paul has in Romans 8. Christ is our stronghold because nothing of infinite, real value could ever be taken from us and the things that are designed to hurt us become the things that God uses to help us become more like Christ.

~

I encourage you to let the light of Christ shine on your troubles wherever you are today. I don't know what kind of misery you're taking into the next morning, or what kind of anxieties you dwell on, or what kinds of questions or tensions you have...you have yours and I have mine. But I know this to be true: as we stay close to our Savior, he will be the light that reveals these things to be what they truly are. Remember that much of our concern is over things that are not real, but only potential troubles. He is our salvation. He has already delivered us from the greatest crisis we would ever face, and that would be the judgment of God. He is our stronghold. Nothing of our joy and happiness can really be taken from us. Our hurts will not last forever in this world, for this world is only temporary. All things come from God and they serve his purposes.

These things can only be true comforts to you if you can share with David the personal nature of his confession. David claims God as *my* light, *my* salvation, *my* stronghold. That's only true if in your heart you believe that Jesus Christ is your Savior and Lord; only then can you say, "He is *my* refuge." If you have yet to humble yourself and confess your sin, repenting and believing in Jesus Christ, I pray now that the Lord would lead you to his love and forgiveness, and that you would find his great mercy for you at the cross of Christ. May God alleviate you of some of your anxieties about what lies ahead. Reflect on what you have learned so far from Psalm 27 and remember all that Christ has been and is for you and trust him. "When I am afraid; I put my trust in you" (Psalm 56:3).

2

SEEKING

One thing have I asked of the Lord, that will I seek after: that I may dwell in the house of the Lord all the days of my life, to gaze upon the beauty of the Lord and to inquire in his temple.
Psalm 27:4

Our lives today are very different from David's. Most of us are not being chased around the countryside by assassins (or at least I don't think so!) The majority of us are not facing armies that are seeking to take our lives, or dodging spears but we do face all sorts of stress, don't we? The Bible is honest about that. Trepidation and distress are our normal human experiences. Jesus said, *"In this world, you will have trouble."* Some of us have known plenty of it. Some of us not as much. But the reality is we can't escape it; we all have our griefs and losses. We are given our individual crosses to bear as we follow Christ. Christ has his face in the wind, and if we're walking at his side, we can only expect the same. So what are we to do? Binge on Netflix, food or shopping, or pause for our ten-minute "relaxation technique" with the latest positive thinking guru? No, instead of searching like so many in the culture do for a technique to either numb ourselves or get a quick fix, we ought to learn how to face the reality that life is full of calamity. We ought to learn how to process our concerns as directed in the Word of God, and that is with a Christian worldview, through the lens of the gospel, through which we relate to God with Christ our Savior. This is what we learned in Chapter 1 by *trusting* God through our trials, firmly believing that we have a heavenly friend and Father who is himself our light, salvation, and stronghold for our deliverance. But are we close enough to our heavenly Father to walk in the glow of his light? David's second, and perhaps most central, spiritual strategy for overcoming fear and anxiety involves seeking the face of God—the nearness of God.

Dwelling In The House Of The Lord

Verse 4 begins with what commentator Peter Craig says is one of the most single-minded statements of purpose to be found anywhere in the Old Testament: "One thing have I asked of the Lord, that will I seek after," says David. Now of all the things that David could ask of God when his life is on the line, it may be surprising to hear what he requests. When his son Absalom has abandoned him, when everything seems to be turning against him, the one thing he seeks is, "that I may dwell in the house of the Lord all the days of my life."

Astonishing! What would be the one thing you and I might desire? How about "Get me out of this? Can you make it all go away, God?" We might seek control or escape, but the one thing David says he seeks is the presence of God. Now look at the structure here in verses 4-6. First of all, verse 4 is the heart of the entire section. It's where the strategy of seeking is found. When he says, "One thing have I asked," that is implying a past tense as well as a present reality. In other words, he is saying, "*One thing I've asked in the past, and which I am still asking right up to this point.*" Then he says, "that will I seek." Note that the Hebrew verb is translated as a continuous future. He is saying that this is his one persistent request and it will be from here on out. So what is his persistent request, past, present, and future? What is it he is seeking? He answers with three infinitive clauses: *to dwell, to gaze,* and *to inquire.* The first clause, "to dwell in the house of the Lord," is the one thing he is seeking; that is, the one thing he seeks "is to dwell in the house of the Lord." The following two clauses *to gaze* and *to inquire* define or explain WHY he wants to dwell there: I want to dwell there that I may gaze and that I may inquire. Now why does David above all else seek to dwell there?

Verse 5 provides the answer: "For he will hide me in his shelter in the day of trouble; he will conceal me under the cover of his tent; he will lift me high upon a rock." David derives tremendous assurance and confidence from the nearness of God. When he dwells in the house of the Lord, he knows the Lord will shelter him, hide him, and set him on firm, solid ground. As a result of this experience, David now says in verse 6, "and now my head shall be lifted up above my enemies, and I will praise God." The product of his assurance is praise and adoration! But in order to get there we must understand what this meant for David in his time.

When David sought to dwell in the house of the Lord above all else, should we understand this literally? Some scholars say we should. David, our shepherd boy turned warrior, they say, was out there fighting his enemies. However, he greatly desired to attend to the services of the tabernacle. Alternatively, perhaps he wished he could be a priest instead of a king. As priest, he could live within the tabernacle precincts, which is what would have been standing as the center of the worship of God for those Israelites at the time. But the problem with thinking of David's desire as being solely a literal desire is that no one ever lived permanently in the tabernacle structure at that time. It was impossible for even a priest to do that. Every priest returned to his own home amongst the Israelites after performing his Levitical duties. Therefore, this desire has to be to some degree inclusive of figurative language, since it literally could not be done. What is it, then, to dwell in the house of the Lord? *It is to be where God's presence is.* For David the tabernacle was where God's manifest presence resided.

He wanted, as commentator Alexander MacLaren says, "*the abiding consciousness of the Divine presence.*"[13] He wanted to consciously grasp God's presence all the time. Or as John Stott says, "*he had a longing to enjoy unbroken communion with God.*"[14] That's what he desired--the one thing above all else. Now we don't want to divorce the physical from the spiritual absolutely. It may very well be that David literally had heightened experiences of God's presence when he attended tabernacle worship. And perhaps he looked back on those times as gloriously joyful. Like the sons of Korah who wrote Psalm 84 in which was declared, "*better is one day in your courts than thousands elsewhere,*" so for David there was a close correlation between an actual place and the spiritual. For us, it might be more akin to the sense that God met us at church on a particular day in a way that he hadn't met us in a long time, and we wish we could just experience that closeness every day. This nearness to God is the one thing David seeks to help him overcome his fears and anxieties in his life. He trusts that consciously being in the presence of God will sustain through the anxieties of literal warfare.

Another verse to consider is in the well-known Psalm 23, the first of the Psalms 23-29 grouping, that all include similar thematic expressions such as receiving God's protection, dwelling in his house, and waiting for his deliverance. In

---

[13] *Maclaren*, 262.

[14] John Stott, *Favorite Psalms: Growing Closer to God,* (Grand Rapids: Baker Books, 2003) 31.

Psalm 23 David says, "surely goodness and mercy shall follow me all the days of my life and I shall dwell in the house of the Lord forever." Now we know that he did not dwell in the house of the Lord physically every day of his life, but his point is similar to what he has made clear in Psalm 27: more than anything else he desired the Lord to walk with him and to be near to his soul. This was David's outlook. This was his experience. This was his heart. He desired an unbroken, conscious communion with God every moment of his life, no matter where he was or what he was doing.

For David, life's fears did not drive him to check out mentally and spiritually, like so many people do in tribulation, but rather, they drove him nearer to God in his heart and soul. If David were alive today, he wouldn't stop going to church and start turning to the bottle, or resorting to drugs, or staying up all night watching Netflix while multi-thread texting, scanning Facebook and eating chocolate. No, David's troubles caused him to lean into the Lord, and oh, that we would learn from his example! There are people who, when troubles come, their normal seat in church sits empty. Isolating oneself during distressing times is often the natural tendency. On the contrary, David would be found in church around the clock if he could. He says, "When fears come, when anxieties come, I *run to* God and God's presence, because here is what I want most, the sense of God's communion with me." How important it is for us to think as David thought, and to desire what David desired, for when troubles come, the Lord's presence is our stability and strength.

To gaze

How does David spiritually arrive at that abiding sense of God's presence and communion? How does this come about? The answer is in the next two infinitives: *to gaze*, and *to inquire*. In the phrase *"to gaze upon the beauty of the Lord,"* the verb *to gaze* means to behold or to look at something with awe. Alexander MacLaren describes it as a "steadfast and penetrating contemplation".[15] It is not just a glance, but rather a contemplation of something to understand something better of it. Some time ago, I was looking at the drawings of M. C. Escher. He has many intriguing ones, but one of his drawings is of multiple sets of stairs and stairways. As I was studying it, I was trying to discern if the stairs were going up or going down. I would follow the stairs down, and they would end up going up! At first, I couldn't quite figure it out but eventually I began to notice how masterfully clever his lines were drawn, to create depth and the illusion that the staircases were traveling in both directions. Gazing intently at something is how we understand more fully the object of our interest. David wants to gaze intently not at a drawing, but at the *beauty* of the Lord. Now the word *beauty* is an interesting word. The noun occurs in the Psalms only once here and once in Psalm 90:17, where it says let the *favor* of the Lord be upon us. The English Standard Version translates *favor* as *beauty*. The New American Standard translates it as *delightfulness,* and the Septuagint, the *pleasantness* of God. I think the Puritan Matthew Henry captures the essence of the word as "God's glorious excellencies".[16]

When David went to the tabernacle, God's glorious attributes were revealed in the ordinances and activities of worship that David would have seen. When he saw the sacrifices, he beheld the justice of God, the holiness of God, and his mercy, compassion, and grace. He saw substitution for his own sins. And when David went to tabernacle, he saw the priests and their garments, and he smelled the aromas and heard the singers and the clanging of the bells. As he was gazing at what he could understand about God through these elements of worship, he saw the beauty of the Lord. He

[15] *Maclaren*, 262.
[16] Matthew Henry, *Matthew Henry's Commentary on the Whole Bible: Complete and Unabridged in One Volume* (Peabody: Hendrickson, 1994), 779.

didn't see rituals for themselves, but through the rituals he saw the display of the attributes of the Lord. And it was the one thing he wanted in his heart, to dwell in the house of the Lord, and to gaze there upon the beauty of God. Think about this: David was captivated by the character of God so vividly though he was given only a shadowy representation of the forgiveness and love of God to come later through Jesus Christ. Yet he was exalting and praising God with the fullest of hearts, and in that way, he overcame his fears. How much more clearly can we behold God's love and beauty today than David could? So much more!

Indeed, we have so much more. We have Christ himself to gaze at. We are told in the book of Hebrews that all the Old Testament rituals were but shadows of the good things to come, and most of it has come in the person of Christ. Like a well-worn mountain pass trail that one travels daily over and over, when we learn to habitually gaze through what we're hearing and reading about Christ, to see the beauties of God, we'll receive that same sense of comfort. Jesus came to make the Father known no longer merely by means of shadows but in fleshly reality: *"And the word became flesh and dwelt among us and we have seen his glory; glory as of the only (*or unique one*) Son from the Father, full of grace and truth"* (John 1:14). The disciples beheld his glory in a way David could only look forward to with the eyes of faith.

Further on in verse 18, John says that no one has seen God at any time, but the only begotten Son, or the unique Son, who comes from the bosom of the Father has explained him. The literal word there is he has *exegeted* him. To exegete is to lead out the meaning of something—to interpret. Jesus has made God known. He's revealed him. John goes on to say, and we "have seen his glory" (John 1:14). Yes, we have so much more to behold in order to understand the beauty of the Lord by simply looking at Jesus. We have the life of Christ presented in the four Gospels. We have the cross. We have an empty tomb and the resurrection; we have Pentecost and the gift of the Holy Spirit. We have the miracles of Christ, his mercy and compassion, all written down for us to behold over and over. We have so much more to gaze at, dear Christian, that we may see the beauty of the Lord. And how is this a great aid in our battle against anxiety?

The struggle against anxiety is a struggle against unbelief and a battle for belief—belief in God as revealed in his Son, the Lord Jesus. Gazing at Christ brings the light of his nature and character into our daily lives. The Puritan Thomas Goodwin described it as "a habitual sight of him." He writes:

> *The indwelling of Christ by faith…is to have Jesus Christ continually in one's eye, a habitual sight of Him. I call it so because a man actually does not always think of Christ; but as a man does not look up to the sun continually, yet he sees the light of it…So you should carry along and bear along in your eye the sight and knowledge of Christ, so that at least a presence of Him accompanies you, which faith makes.* [17]

Take a moment now, dear reader, to gain a clearer and deeper sight of Christ. Open your bible to Hebrews 1 and within just the first 8 verses you will see that:

Jesus Christ is the Son of God.

Jesus Christ is the greatest and clearest word from God to you.

Jesus Christ is the heir of all things.

Jesus Christ is the one through whom God created the world.

Jesus Christ is the radiance of the glory of God.

---

[17] Thomas Goodwin, *Works,* Vol. 2, (Grand Rapids: Reformation Heritage Books, 2006), 411.

Jesus Christ is the exact imprint of God's nature.

Jesus Christ upholds the universe by the word of his power.

Jesus Christ made purification for your sins.

Jesus Christ is now seated at the right hand of Majesty on high.

Jesus Christ is superior to the angels as he is worshipped by them.

Jesus Christ is enthroned forever and ever over the kingdom of God.

To inquire

The next infinitive is *to inquire* in his temple. This is a difficult verb to translate. It's been translated by some as *to divine*, or to seek a word or oracle from God. In biblical times, kings would go into the tabernacle (later the temple) and seek a word from God. Imagine Joshua going into the tent of meeting and asking of the Lord, "Shall we attack?" Joshua was *inquiring*, trying to *divine* a word from God. But I agree with E.W. Hengstenburg, an Old Testament Hebrew scholar, that it is best translated here as meditate, as the New American Standard version of the Bible renders it.[18] The context here is not so much David seeking *to divine* an oracle of the Lord, but rather, after gazing at the beauty of the Lord, he is seeking *to meditate* upon him. It is more natural to translate the Hebrew term this way in this context. Deep reflecting and meditation naturally follow after gazing intently upon God's nature (Psalm 1:1-2). As David contemplated what he saw in the tabernacle worship services, he wanted to spend some time sitting down and ruminating upon the thoughts of God.

---

[18] E. W. Hengstenburg, *Commentary on the Book of Psalms,* found in Clarks Foreign Theological Library Vol. 1, (Edinburgh: T. & T. Clark, 1869), 455.

He had a desire to "chew on" the thoughts of God in his mind and heart. That's meditation. Biblical meditation is not the emptying of your mind, but the filling of it. It is filling it over and over and over, chewing the cud like a cow and trying to penetrate deeper in your comprehension of what God is saying in his word. What is God revealing about himself in this? What do these Scriptures show me about the character of God? What is his mercy like in these passages? His love? And I'll say this is not only true of David, but also of you and me: *a believer receives power to face their fears and challenges from the contemplation of God.*

To contemplate God in Christ as we have him, is to see God's grace. And to see grace with the eyes of faith is to receive grace; and to receive grace is to receive power—and with it, the courage to be unafraid and trusting in the Lord. That's how it works. The gospel is not only a one-time revelation of grace, but a constant channel of grace enabling us to reflect on who God is for us in Christ. The gospel therefore is not just letting us see that grace but enabling us to receive it *continually*. At that very moment that your soul is filled up and receives grace, it also receives power. That's why Christians, true believers, love the preaching of the gospel over and over; they need power to persevere in this life once again.

The power of grace comes from *meditatively seeing* grace in the gospel, otherwise Paul would not say what he said to Timothy, his protégé, in 2 Timothy 2:1: "Be *being* strengthened by the grace that is in Christ Jesus our Lord" (my translation). He is declaring to Timothy that there is grace to be found as he reflects upon Jesus and who he is, and on his fellowship and communion with him. Paul says, as you receive that grace, Timothy, you'll be spiritually strengthened to face challenges. Paul needed to remind him of this because we're shown in the first chapter in 2 Timothy that apparently Timothy had withdrawn spiritually and had to some degree suffered for the sake of Christ already. So Paul encouraged Timothy saying, "Join me in this. Don't be afraid. You have to face this and you need to walk with me in this. This is how you will do it, Timothy, by being strengthened by the grace that is in Christ Jesus, our Lord. Gaze and then meditate. Meditate upon who he is and be strengthened." As Nehemiah states, "The joy of the Lord is your strength" (Neh. 8:10). To receive the joy of the Lord and the joy of our salvation, we must once again reflect on the beauty of God in Christ as revealed to us in the cross. Then we will have fresh strength to face our fears yet another day.

David goes on to say in verse 5 that when he is in that spiritual frame of mind, God "will hide me in his shelter in the day of trouble. He will conceal me under the cover of his tent. He will lift me high upon a rock." In essence, David is affirming 2 Timothy 2:1. He had received power and the comfort of assurance through God's grace. This verse also describes David's psychological state, his emotions of the mind and heart. This is what he felt. The verses create a picture of David hastening inwardly into the house of God even though he had not literally run into the tabernacle. He refers to God's protection in these few verses as house, shelter, cover, tent, and temple. When we see the word *tent*, we must remember the culture of David's time. If you were a tired traveler from the Old Testament era and you came into someone's tent, your host would graciously receive you and provide for you. It was their cherished custom to provide a devoted protection for you. Consider Lot, Abraham's cousin, who even offered his own daughters to the gathering mob of men in order to protect his visitors. David is saying, "In my soul I've come into the house of the Lord himself, and suddenly my soul isn't as troubled. He is protecting me, and he is devoted to comforting me." This sounds similar to Philippians 4:7 where Paul says, 'the peace of God, which surpasses all understanding, will guard your hearts and your minds in Christ Jesus." When we draw this close to God and are in communion with him, it will be as if we have been brought into his own tent, and he protects and surrounds our souls. He lifts us above all these vexations that have been consuming us and driving our decisions.

Dwelling in God's tent will naturally result in not only peace from all our fears but an exuberant joy that is full of praise to God. Verse 6 states, "And now my head shall be lifted up above my enemies all around me, and I will offer in his tent sacrifices with shouts of joy; I will sing and make melody to the Lord." David is telling us that the way to overcome fears is *to persevere this far in the pursuit of communion with God.* David doesn't just survive fears. Like the apostle Paul, David struggled with all God's energy that "powerfully worked within him" to get to the place where he could praise God exuberantly in the midst of fears (Col. 1:29).

Beginning with reflection, he walked through contemplation, to meditation, to a sense of assurance, and then finally ended in a place of adoration and freeing joy in God. David can shout this to God, "God, you are my refuge," and do it with praises! David could smile, David could laugh, and David could continue his days free from fear though the situation with Saul or his son, Absalom were still difficult. In the words of the Puritan William Law, "*Assurance has a joyful voice.*"[19] Finding that assurance, whether or not our circumstances change, is where many of us struggle, because we've not drawn near to the house of the Lord. But when we've hastened to the Lord in our souls and gazed, and we've inquired and meditated, assurance will follow. God has promised this. And after that comes praise, because assurance has a joyful voice.

---

[19] William Law, "Psalm 27," *Grace Gems*, accessed March 22, 2020, https://www.gracegems.org/LAW/psalm_27.htm

Cherish the Lord

Let's look at what's spiritually going on in our hearts when we are struggling to find that assurance of peace and freedom. As I commented above, many of us struggle to find what David did. What David teaches us in verses 4-6 is that when your relationship with Jesus is the one thing you seek above all else, you can overcome all fear because no one and nothing can touch that hope in the Lord. However, the reverse is true, too. You become vulnerable to anxieties when the things that you cherish the most in life are *not* your relationship with Christ because those things *will* be touched. And it's not a matter of *if* they will be touched, but *when* and *how*.

We live in a culture today that is extraordinarily mindful of being healthy. There are so many books, articles, blogs, websites, and whole stores devoted to the selling of products and diets that will assure you of your lasting health and vitality if you follow their protocols. Unfortunately, I have a bomb to drop here. If your health is the true center of your life, the one thing you cherish above everything else, I can tell you that someday it's going to crumble, and eventually, give out. If that's what you *live* for (no pun intended), you must realize that someday life in this body for you will end. Your soul will depart and your body will deteriorate. If it is your wealth that you cherish above all else, you will move on from this life and your wealth will be given to others. Whatever you revere and hold as dearest to your heart, there you are vulnerable to anxieties because you are cherishing something that's perishable. Everything EXCEPT Christ is subject to deterioration in this life. Only Jesus is the same yesterday, today and forever.

Jesus Himself instructs us in the same manner as David. When we come to the New Covenant, we hear Jesus echo the same call to a higher worship and more lasting treasure. David said, "One thing I seek," and Jesus says, "Seek ye first the Kingdom of God," and (I'm paraphrasing here) "all these other things you tend to cherish will be added to you in proportion as God wants." Jesus explains how at the deepest level, the struggle becomes a matter of what our hearts worship (or desire): He said,

> *Do not lay up for yourselves treasures on earth where moth and rust destroy and where thieves break in and steal, but lay up for yourselves treasures in heaven where neither moth nor rust destroys and where thieves do not break in and steal. For where your treasure is there your heart is also. (Matt 6:19-21)*

Christ desires us to treasure him for he is the only thing that will never leave us alone and disillusioned with an empty promise of lasting happiness and peace. All material wealth, earthly relationships, personal achievements, longevity of health and power promise eternal satisfaction (and one can say freedom from unhappiness, like fear and anxiety) but delivers nothing. We become more fretful and burdened with the cares of "keeping" and maintaining these lesser treasures. And we will often see these transient things fade before our eyes within this life, and others dwindle at the end of our life when we must leave them behind to face the Creator of ALL lasting joy. But when our hearts' chief desire is Christ himself, to grow in communion and knowledge of him, not only does the Lord provide these lesser treasures according to his sovereign will and for our blessing, but we will also find our hearts naturally begin to loosen our grip on these "perishable cherishables," no longer needing them for our sense of security. In this way our fears of losing them, like the retreating ocean pools at low tide, slacken and ebb away.

It is good to acknowledge as well that our struggle as Christians today is typically not the cherishing of something evil or wrong over cherishing Christ. For instance, is it right to cherish your children? Yes, absolutely. They are a gift of God and we should cherish our children, BUT if we cherish them to the depth that they are becoming the center of our life, and all our joy and happiness is being bound with them, then that good thing has become a bad thing for us because it is now the "functional god" of our life. Though we are confessing Jesus as our Lord, really our lord is the happiness derived from our children doing well in life and becoming all that we really hoped they could be. Or we may feel as though we cannot live without them, for the joy of their companionship and existence is what makes us most satisfied. We hold on to them tightly, and I have seen many times how difficult it can be for parents of older children to let go of their grip of control and joy-seeking from their children's relationships with them. This ultimately is difficult for both the parent and the child. It puts an unbearable pressure on the child to either live to fulfill their parents' happiness or they feel stifled by the idolatry the parents have of them. It can look different to different families and relationships. The point is, we become full of anxiety because we often look to the blessings of God in our lives, like our relationships and other good, wholesome gifts of God, instead of God himself, to deliver our lasting fulfillment in this life. And we are not in control of these other people in our life nor of our things. The Lord is--and we can substitute any *multitude* of things in replacement of Christ as our treasure.

Consider the story of Mary and Martha. Jesus came to the house of his friend Lazarus. His two sisters Mary and Martha were also there. Martha was consumed with a *good* thing; there were guests in their home. Scripture teaches us that we have to be hospitable, but Martha was *consumed* with hospitality. In Luke 10, we read that they welcomed Jesus into their home, and Mary sat at the Lord's feet listening to his teaching. She was gazing and inquiring, but Martha was distracted with much serving (which perhaps didn't look like much outward sinning). She was serving the disciples of Jesus. That seems like a good thing, doesn't it? It does until you discern the better offer that she had to occupy her heart. She had a choice, of course. The choice was this: listen to the Son of God who had set foot in her house, or be thought of well by others through her serving. She chose being distracted with much serving. Martha went to the Lord and said, "Lord, do you not care that my sister has left me to serve alone? Do you see the pile of dishes? Tell her to help me."

Listen to our Lord's sweet answer: "Martha, Martha, you are anxious and troubled about many things, not just the dishes." You see, he knew Martha's heart. He was letting her know that this was indicative of her. "This is characteristic of you, Martha. This is what you're like. You're anxious, you're troubled about many things, but one thing is necessary." Remember what David said? "This is the *one thing* I seek." And the one thing Martha sought wasn't Christ himself. Jesus said, "There is only one thing that's actually necessary, Martha; Mary has chosen the good portion which shall not be taken away from her." We see in those statements the deep compassion of Christ, who was telling her and us that if we seek him as that one necessary thing, through our walk with him and our knowledge of him, he will be there to bless us. He won't send us away. There's nothing better you could be doing. And so many of us are troubled by so many things; good things that have become the main thing, good things that have displaced the one thing that is truly necessary, which is our communion with Christ, our fellowship with him. Sibbes insightfully notes, "It is the nature of the soul, when it is upon many things, it can do nothing well."[20] This reminds me of that well-known Christian song, the chorus of which so many of us know by heart:

---

[20] *Sibbes,* location 183.

Turn your eyes upon Jesus

Look full in His wonderful face

And the things of earth will grow strangely dim

In the light of his glory and grace.

The "things of earth" that will diminish include not just earthly possessions, but also our fears. As we begin to sit at the feet of Jesus to gaze and inquire and to cherish, we, along with Martha, will relinquish our frantic hold on the things of this world, and come to find that sweet contentment and peace in the face of our loving Savior and God.

How Is This Done?

So how do I do this? How do I practically keep Christ in the center? It's a struggle for me even though I study the Bible every week as part of my pastoral role in our church. It's a spiritual exercise for all of us. One example of a man who excelled in keeping his heart focused on Christ is George Mueller who was a contemporary of Charles Spurgeon back in the 1800s. He started a handful of orphanages which he sustained through prayer alone. Prayer was a means of grace that Mueller grew an extraordinary capacity to lay hold of by faith. His biography had a powerful impact on me as a young believer. In one of his biographical writings, he shares that early on he wanted to pray every morning after he got dressed. So he did, for many years. But then he discovered something that caused him to change that desire. He began to see more clearly than ever that the first and greatest primary business to which he ought to attend every day was to have his soul enjoying the presence and favor of God through his word even before prayer.

He acknowledged that if he went out to serve people, yet was not being made happy in the Lord, and not being nurtured and strengthened in his inner man day by day, all of his service might not be attended to in a right spirit. This is not to say that prayer is not a means of communion with God and an appropriate (and commanded) discipline to excel in our walks with Christ. But he felt instinctively, by the Spirit, that to move his soul into a happy state, and to keep his inner man nourished, the most important thing he had to do was to give himself to the reading of the Word of God, and to meditate upon it. Before this time, his habitual practice to give himself to prayer after having dressed in the morning had been half the coin, so to speak. But in first reading the Scriptures, in so doing his heart was experientially comforted, encouraged, warned, reproved, and instructed. That's a Puritan way of describing being in *communion* with the Lord. It is as if Mueller was saying, "David is right; the one thing in life really is communion with the Lord, so what I did is this: I read my Scriptures every day, and not only did I read them, but I contemplated them until I felt that my heart was moved, until I had met with the Lord. I didn't just simply check them off a chart that I had read today's verses. I dwelt and meditated, then I prayed upon those Scriptures, and I was strengthened ten-fold."

As Christians, we begin to praise God. We begin to experience God in that sense of delighting in who he is for us in Christ. Like Mueller says, "contemplating until my heart is moved, until I see something of the love of God, and I experience it."[21] We react to God's truth, starting to ask questions like, "How should I change in light of the beauty of God? What should I think now? How should I face my troubles in light of what I'm seeing here in front of me?"

Let me illustrate this another way. Not all of us are labelled artistic, *per se*, but we all do possess different ways of

---

[21] George Mueller, *Autobiography of George Mueller: A Million and a Half in Answer to Prayer,* Ebook, (London: 3rd Edition, 1837, Monergism), March 18, 2020,
https://www.monergism.com/thethreshold/sdg/muller/Autobiography%20of%20George%20Muller%20-%20George%20Muller.pdf

expressing creativity, such as music, cooking, and so forth. So picture someone you love, perhaps your child or perhaps your parent or a close friend, writing a piece of music or painting a vibrant watercolor landscape, and they bring it to you as a gift. As you listen to the music or see the painting for the first time, you thank them with a smile, and under their pleased eye you begin to analyze the gift. You remark, "Oh, look at that. I can see the way you did that. That's a good brush stroke." Or "That's an amazing refrain you crafted! What cadence! Oh, well, you actually have one beat more than the measure is long here. You can't do that." You critique and observe, and then you move to the second stage of contemplation where you start to see something *of them* coming out of the piece. You now say, "Wow, that sounds really tender," or "That shows great enthusiasm!" Perhaps you notice how dark the colors are in the landscape, a reflection of the mood of the artist or the tone they were trying to capture. You're reacting to their creation and their expression of what they felt on the inside as they crafted it. You realize you're getting to know them through this gift, and then you've moved to the last element, to delight. "I am just blown away by you," you say in awe. Or you exclaim, "My heart is so warmed by what you've written, by what you've done! Thank you for such a great gift."

~

There is but one thing that we ought to seek: to contemplate God and to know him. And in order to do that, we must gaze, so that we can then meditate and inquire. Some of you perhaps reading this might be thinking, "That just sounds too involved." My friend, you and I live in a quick-fix, instant cappuccino society...the sound-bite generation. David will tell us at the end of the Psalm to *wait* (gasp!) for the Lord. This is a habit that must be developed, and there are no short cuts to establishing it. Indeed all habits must be continuously and consistently carved deeply into our daily routines until they become second-nature. When we hear this, we are tempted to balk at the process and say, "Listen, Tony, I've got bills to pay at the end of next week. I don't have time to sit and think like this." But I write to urge and to testify, both from my personal experience of this life in Christ and from his word, and also from my heart's desire for your joy and freedom from fear: *you need more of Christ in your soul than you have of your anxieties*. I don't know what's going to happen at the end of next week, or whether or not you'll be able to pay your bills, but I do know that if you have more of Christ in your heart, you'll be able to better face whatever is coming regardless.

Here is a very good poem by Paul Tripp that I want to leave with you, and it is based on Psalm 27:4. (As an important side note, let me assure you, Tripp is no gnostic; meaning, he does not think that material things are evil, and spiritual things are good. He is simply emphasizing that the one thing David sought is best for us to also seek).

One thing,
One thing,
One thing!
It's hard to imagine
One thing
When I seem to be attracted
to so many things.
It is a continuing
struggle.
It is a daily
battle.
It is my constant
war.
The world of the physical
attracts me
excites me
magnetizes me
addicts me.
I confuse consumption
with satisfaction.
I confuse satisfied senses
with true joy.
I confuse a stomach that is full
with a heart at rest.
Sometimes I would rather have
my appetites satisfied
than a grace filled heart.
Sometimes I would rather hold
the physical
than have the eyes of my heart
be filled
with the beauty of
the spiritual.
I am tired of only seeing
what
my physical eyes
can see.
I want eyes
to see
what
cannot be seen.
I am tired of craving
people

possessions
locations
circumstances
positions
experiences
appearances...
Somewhere in my heart
I know that only you
satisfy.
Deep in my heart
I want you to be
enough.
I must quit
moving
running
driving
pursuing
consuming.
I need to
stop.
I need to
be quiet.
I need to sit
in the seat of grace
and wait
and wait
until these blind eyes
see
until this cold heart
craves
the one beauty that
satisfies
the one beauty that
is You.[22]

---

[22] Paul Tripp, "Psalm 27: One Thing," (Paul Tripp Ministries), October 26, 2007, http://paultrippministries.blogspot.com/2007/10/one-thing.html

What is pressuring its way into the epicenter of your life? Identify it. Sit down this week. Sit long enough and quietly enough to gaze and to meditate until Christ comes back to the center.

Whom Shall I Fear?

3

ASKING

Hear, O LORD, when I cry aloud; be gracious to me and answer me!
Psalm 27:7

How great a privilege is prayer. Think about this. Whether we are simply experiencing a moment of indecisiveness or one of the hardest, deepest trials of our life, we can talk to God about it. Whether we have a small question or a life-changing question, we can ask him. Philippians 4:6-7 says,

> *"...do not be anxious about anything, but in everything by prayer and supplication with thanksgiving let your requests be made known to God. And the peace of God, which surpasses all understanding, will guard your hearts and your minds in Christ Jesus."*

The term "to guard" refers to the protection of a garrison or a group of soldiers. That's a tremendous promise. But it is found only in Christ Jesus. Paul says we can experience this heart-protecting peace if we possess Christ. We can speak with him, and the God of the universe hears us.

We are told again in Hebrews to "then with confidence draw near to the throne of grace that we may receive mercy and find grace to help in time of need" (Hebrews 4:16). Whereas David would bring sacrifices into the tent of the Lord and pray through the shadows of tabernacle worship, we have a clearer picture of our great high priest who has passed through the heavens. We can worship and pray with a fuller knowledge of who he is, seeing his finished work on the cross, and triumph over death via his resurrection. Jesus the Son of God is there at the right hand of God interceding on our behalf. And he understands, for he has experienced our sufferings. Oh, the privilege and the power of prayer for us as New Covenant believers!

This is where many of us fall short in our battle against anxiety. We struggle with fears because we fail to pray. Not only do we fail to grow in the *quality* of our prayer life, but we just fail to pray at all. Or perhaps we lack confidence in prayer. It is my hope that God will help give each of us greater confidence in prayer, appreciate the privilege of it, and then elevate our practice of it as we adopt David's approach to prayer as a third weapon in our arsenal against anxiety. We will see how quickly David flew to prayer and how highly he considered it, even though all he knew of God was seen dimly through the Old Covenant promise of One to come. David still believed rightly he had access to the living God, and because he believed this, he could live fearlessly in a troubling world.

As David's psalm culminates at this high peak of prayer for himself and his safety, there are three qualities to it in verses 7-10 that gave strength to his faith and courage. We will leave the specific requests he makes in verses 11 and 12 for the next chapter. Before looking at the qualities of his plea it is prudent to notice the distance closing between him and the Lord as he draws nearer to God with great urgency. There is an abrupt change in Verse 7. Shifting from singular pronouns to the second person, he is now addressing God directly. He petitions, "Hear, O LORD...be gracious to me..." This is a prayer and it is one that carries all the way through Verse 12. There are also abrupt mood shifts within it. He goes from the heights of confidence ("...my head shall be lifted up above my enemies..."), to the depths of despair. He cries out, "Hide not your face from me. Turn not your servant away in anger..." As mentioned before, it is this great contrast that has led some critics of the Bible to conclude these are two psalms that are stuck together haphazardly and hence unreliable. But as I have previously argued this is indeed one psalm that reflects David's current circumstances as well as the reality of his turbulent emotions as he seeks refuge from the Lord at that time.

We see this growing uneasiness drawing nearer to David as the psalm unfolds. Verse 3, though not hypothetical, gave a sense of a greater gap between himself and the enemy: "Though an army encamp against me...though war arise against me..." He speaks of it with an objective voice— observing it and seeing his situation as dark but not yet speaking to the Lord directly of it. But now in Verse 7, he launches into present tense experience—and he is definitely seeking God's attention! "Hear, O Lord, when I cry aloud; be gracious to me and answer me!" It is as if David cries out, "God, I'm wrestling my way through this right now! I'm scared! Help me! Hear my prayers!" This is the here and now for David. You don't cry for relief if nothing is happening. We have covered the arc of his plight with Saul and Absalom, and so we can gather why he naturally felt this way.

Earnest Engagement

The first quality of his prayer life was he asked with an earnest impudence. Read again of the direct, emotional, zealous language in verse 7: "Hear, O LORD, when I cry aloud; be gracious to me and answer me!" Do you hear that? *Hear...be gracious...answer me.* All three are imperatives or commands. Wow. Commanding Yahweh, the LORD? The great I AM?

Yes, he speaks to Him directly like that. Like in so many of his other psalms, David says, "I am crying aloud!" He's not just thinking his prayers but he's speaking them audibly. There's something to be said about praying out loud. When we pray out loud, it involves our entire person, our bodies and minds, in our prayer life. We would say today that David was "all in" on his prayer life. He's on his knees, or he's pacing his cave where he has hidden his men while Saul relentlessly scours towns and countryside searching for him. He's praying with such an all-encompassing focus that his men know not to disturb him as they hear his voice at morning, noon and night. He's praying fervently and he's not just mumbling it. He believes only God can help him. He asserts to God himself that he is going to cry out to him and he wants God to listen. So many of our prayers can sound like little indecisive chats. It's why so many prayer meetings die out because everyone's falling asleep. Our prayers can become like little chats at Starbucks or at a Peet's coffee counter. A half-distracted, half-hearted "hi-how-are-you-oh-I-don't-know-should-I-get-this-or-that…" and perhaps a comment or two about the summer heat wave recently and then we walk away. No real desire to engage completely.

Our prayer life, especially at critical times in our lives, shouldn't just sound like a chat at the counter of Peet's coffee. It's being engaged, fully engaged, with the living God. David is all in. He would desire that our prayer meetings kindle and spark into flame with more bold, direct zeal and that is exactly what Jesus exhibited. The Son of God encouraged us in these types of prayers. When he was ministering, the disciples came up to him and said, "Teach us to pray." And he taught the Lord's Prayer, saying, "You speak like this: 'Give us this day our daily bread.'" He modeled that direct address to God in heaven. Indeed, God *desires* you to address him face to face. He wants you to have that kind of confidence through the cross of Christ. "God, we need your sustenance. Give us bread today." Luke chapter 11 records the Lord's Prayer in its entirety and then immediately afterward records Jesus's parable which he gave to illustrate this familiarity with God we ought to have as His children. Luke 11:5-6 states that Jesus told his disciples, after he taught them the Lord's Prayer, "…which of you who has a friend will go to him at midnight and say to him, 'Friend, lend me three loaves, for a friend of mine has arrived on a journey, and I have nothing to set before him.'?"

Jesus is implying you *should* have friends like that whom you could ask, and you should be willing to ask them. In Verse 7 he goes on to say, "…and he (the neighbor or friend) will answer him from within, 'Do not bother me; the door is now shut, and my children are with me in bed. I cannot get up and give you anything.' "I tell you," said Jesus…"though he will not get up and give him anything because he is his friend, yet because of his impudence he will rise and give him whatever he needs."

The word *impudence* there is the key word that we ought to take to heart. It's boldness. It's not about persistence—at least not in this parable. The ESV translation uses the word *impudence* which is much better than the New American Standard that says, "…because of his perseverance…" Perseverance is a tertiary meaning of that word. The word *impudence* gets right to the heart of what Jesus is illustrating. It is because of his temerity that the man's friend will arise and give him whatever he needs. Jesus encouraged, "Ask and it will be given to you; seek, and you will find; knock, and it will be opened to you. For everyone who asks receives, and the one who seeks finds, and to the one who knocks it will be opened" (Matthew 7:7-8). What Jesus desired was for his people to presume upon their God to hear their prayers and to come to him with no reservations. Because of Christ, we have unfiltered access to the throne room and there, where God dwells, our prayers on earth are heard. Arndt and Gingrich, one of the best-known Greek lexicons, states these parables illustrate the "shamelessness" that he's asking us to pray with.[23] This characterization should resonate in our prayers.

Have you ever lived in a neighborhood where the unwritten (or perhaps written!) regulation was to keep all outdoor activity and loud music to a minimum by 10p.m. or so? When we intrude upon other people's tranquility at an inappropriate hour, we call it "disturbing the peace". If one of us were to walk over to our next-door neighbor's house at 3a.m. in the morning and knock loudly, over and over, until everyone in the house was woken up and fumbling for lights, that's impudence—to ask, seek, and knock at 3a.m. Well, the infinite and all-powerful God neither slumbers nor sleeps. He is never tucked away to be left alone and undisturbed for a few hours. Go speak to him. We might ask, how is this rude behavior acceptable? How can Jesus teach us to do this? Well, the point is that this is not how you would treat a stranger, but a friend. This is the way you would address a friend whom you know will meet your need and Christ wants you to understand that he has made God in heaven your friend. He has made him your confidante and he desires you to have this earnest impudence in your prayer life. He wants you to feel the liberty of having God himself as a friend like this. When we begin to understand the freedom we possess of audacious and fearless prayer to God, it is one of the most beautiful blessings we can take full advantage of—and with no shame.

I remember when Sheri and I were raising our kids during

---

[23] William Arndt et al., *A Greek-English Lexicon of the New Testament and Other Early Christian Literature* (Chicago: University of Chicago Press, 2000), 63.

the first church plant we were involved with several years ago. During that season we had the privilege of close friends being involved with it, some whom we are still in close contact with even today. We would call up one of these friends in the middle of the night blurting out, "Do you have any children's Tylenol?" There'd be a pause (probably because they were still waking up!) and then a sleepy, "Yeah, we've got it. We'll meet you out front." Of course, back then stores weren't open around the clock like many are now. Christ teaches us as his children that we have a friend in heaven whose door is open to us every moment of every day of our lives. Andrew Murray said, "prayer is an appeal to the friendship of God."[24] Let us appeal without delay, without hesitation.

Another reason to develop an earnest impudence in your prayer life is because prayer is a laborious, spiritual exercise. If we become lazy about our prayers, we spiritually (and even often literally) sleep through praying. We ought never to falter so. Our prayer life ought to be habitually sincere and punctuated with frequent expressions of ardent devotion and thankful praise to our God. Of course, our daily requests and needs should also be laid before him, with a single-minded faith that he can sustain us however he chooses. If we never have moments in our life where we sound more like we're preaching than praying, calling out with our fullest voice to reach the rafters of heaven, then the result will be a sluggish prayer life. Prayer requires spiritual energy! Vigor! Prayer requires action, our bodies active, our minds alert, our hearts engaged in the battle. Indeed, Paul tells us that prayer is wrestling against the forces of darkness and spiritual wickedness in the heavenly places (Eph. 6:12).

In fact, Jesus teaches us that prayer is wrestling against

---

[24] Andrew Murray, *With Christ in the School of Prayer,* (Grand Rapids, MI: Zondervan, 1983) 37.

our *own* flesh. In the dark of night, in the midst of the garden of Gethsemane, spirits were willing, but the flesh was weak, and Jesus lamented that the disciples could not just stay up one hour to pray with him. "Peter, John, wake up! Evil is near, but our God is nearer. Come and pray!" When I think of Jesus's zeal at Gethsemane and about Peter's failure to have it at that moment when our Savior needed it most, it makes my heart yearn for Peter and for myself to own an earnest impudence to pray zealously, so that we might overcome our own tiredness. It is a spiritual discipline. And often when we grow dismissive or lukewarm about prayer, God stirs us up by sending circumstances into our lives that give rise to fear, and straining under the weight of this burden, we finally sound like David in Psalm 27. "Hear me! I'm crying out! Help me, O God!" We finally wake up and begin to storm the gates of heaven, as we should at all times because life is a spiritual battlefield every moment of every day. From here to the grave, we are the church militant. This is wartime, dear friends. Awaken to the skirmishes clashing about you and join the call to prayer.

Consider the testimony of David Brainerd, a young missionary to the Indians in early America. He lived a very short life, yet one characterized by a tremendous prayer life. His journals were preserved, and he notes on one occasion he was in such anguish and pleaded with so much earnestness and importunity that when he rose from his knees, he felt "extremely weak and overcome and I could hardly walk, sweat ran down my face and body."[25] That's what he looked like when he finished praying. He sounds like Jesus who sweated great drops of blood pleading to the Father. Have our own hearts ever been so fervent? Let it be so. Fears and anxieties are overcome as we pound on the door of heaven

---

[25] Jonathon Edwards, ed., *The Life and Diary of David Brainerd*, (1817, repr., Grand Rapids, MI: 1999), 173.

and pray with an earnest impudence.

Hastening Heaven

The second quality of David's prayer life that helped him overcome his fears was asking with a *responsive immediacy.* Verse 8 states, "Seek my face. My heart says to you, your face, LORD, do I seek." In the original Hebrew this verse literally translates to this: "of you has said my heart, seek my face." What do we make of this small phrase? This is a precious, personal dialogue between David and God. We discover David recalling to the Lord what the Lord had already spoken to him: "Lord, you have said to my heart, 'Seek my face.' And so I say to you, Lord, 'Your face, LORD, do I seek.'" Seeking God's face again implies seeking the presence of God and communion with Him. But we ought to notice that this is David "jumping up" in response to God's call to him in his life. It is like Samuel as a young boy, hearing the voice of the Lord crying, "Samuel, Samuel!" asking for him. Samuel swiftly lifted his head, instantly replying "Speak Lord, for your servant is here!" (1 Samuel 3:10). The prayer that overcomes fear and anxieties--prayers that lead us into the presence of God and give us confidence, are those that respond to God entreating us with an eager readiness: "You have called me Lord, and I am here."

I imagine David reflecting back on his experiences of tabernacle worship, remembering times of conversation with God in prayer, and he hears God speaking to him right then on the battlefield too. When he felt God's presence near, or he met God in his word, even as he charged the lines of battle and engaged in physical conflict, his heart was tuned to God's voice. He was ready to react and to respond to the Lord's call. John Calvin said, "As we hear God presenting himself to us, let us cordially reply."[26] God is calling out to us in the troubles of life! Let us turn to him immediately, without delay. He delights in speaking with us much as we do in our closest earthly relationships with one another. A mother drawing near to her daughter and spending time together, sharing worries and burdens from one side, and imparting wisdom and comfort from the other. An old friend reunites with another and the evening draws long on past stories, recent adventures, and reflections on lives lived out so far. Our desire to communicate with one another as people created in the image of God reflects the heart of God as the Communicator-Initiator in our lives. "Come to me," he says. "Let us reason (speak, work this out) together" (Isaiah 1:18). "You will seek me and find me." (Jer. 29:13).

The moment you are born again, that's God inviting you to know him and speak with him. Henry opines, "He calls us, by the whispers of his Spirit to and with our spirits, to seek his face. He calls us by his word…and by special providences merciful and afflictive."[27] Note that he says that in addition to his word, God often calls us to seek his face and prayerfully respond to him "by special providences." These providences break upon us in the form of merciful blessings (perhaps he blesses you materially or relationally or spiritually) or as merciful afflictions (he sends tribulation into our lives). In both these instances, "God calls us to seek his face in our conversion to him and in our converse with him."[28]

Which of the two categories is the louder "horn of the Lord" in our lives? C.S. Lewis memorably answers this question with the notion that pain is God's "megaphone." At

---

[26] John Calvin and James Anderson, *Commentary on the Book of Psalms*, vol. 1 (Bellingham, WA: Logos Bible Software, 2010), 457.

[27] *Henry,* 779.

[28] *Ibid.,* 779.

first, God may call you with his soft whispers in your spirit, and then he may speak to you through his word, sometimes boldly, sometimes loudly. But often times, if we still haven't "gotten up" from our doings (or put our phones down!) and met him in humble prayer, he sends pain ("Have I got your attention now?"). It is God's trumpet. He says, "Stop. Look up. I am here." David tuned his spirit to consistently hear God's voice. He heard his voice in every season of his life, from the fields as a young shepherd boy strumming his harp to the great halls of his kingly palace as he walked its beautiful courts. But perhaps he heard his voice the loudest and clearest when his life was brimming with pain. Saul's persecution, his own repentance after Bathsheba, the death of his child, the betrayal of Absalom…at these times God's megaphone call to David was heavy and clear. In the history of Israel, of course, pain was a common experience. When they grew deaf to God, he would send tribulation. Under Jeremiah the prophet he told them that they would be in captivity in Babylon for 70 years. Talk about a wake-up call! Mercifully, the Lord shared with them that "When 70 years are completed for Babylon, I will visit you…" And when those years are completed, Israel would finally look up with ready hearts and he says, "Then you will call upon me" (Jeremiah 29:12). There's a communion of our souls with the heart of God when God uses affliction in this way to bring us into deeper fellowship with him. When God afflicts us, he visits us with mercy, and in drawing near to him we will prayerfully call upon him and God will hear us and respond. Indeed, God has promised, "You will seek me and find me when you seek me with all your heart" (Jeremiah 29:13).

Are you hearing the voice of Christ? Do you hear God addressing you? I hope you come to understand that the very circumstances you find yourself in, whether pleasant or distressing, is God's saying, "Come talk with me about this!" In the New Testament, Jesus teaches us that we have a standing invitation: "The door is there. I hold the key.

There's no price for entry because I paid it. It's paid in full. So ask, seek, and knock." God promises to respond in love and mercy as our Heavenly Father. He desires to save and to respond to you. David immediately answered God's invitation to seek his face with a verbal reciprocation of trustful love. Too often our response to God's invitation "Seek My face" is "Why are you letting this happen to me? Why is this going on? Why do you allow such things to come into my life?" The answer may very well be that God has brought this particular thing or event into our lives because we have not been habitually coming to him through our normal spiritual disciplines. When he sends events into our lives to gather our attention, for some of us the first thing we do is start questioning the problem of evil. If God is good and almighty, why is he letting this into my life? I must advise that weighing the problem of evil is not the best reaction in times like that. The best response is David's response—an immediate, humble eagerness to seek the Lord and his presence. And of course, to seek his aid. The Lord is saying, "Seek my face." David's response is "Your face, Lord, do I seek." He says, "Here I am and I'm here with an ardent impudence. I'm ready to talk to you right now."

This might happen while you're driving on the road (Please don't close your eyes!). Or it might happen while you're at home or when you're at work. When it does, just speak out loud to the Lord and lay it all before him. To me, it is a great thing when I walk into church on Sundays and I see people praying with each other. Someone sees a brother or sister in Christ and learns of some pressing burden, and right then and there God's face is sought. Recently, we had a visitor who sent a note to us in the church office to let us know how just seeing people praying out loud on the church grounds blessed them immensely. When things that give rise to grief come to bear upon us, it doesn't mean that God is absent or distant, but rather God is right there knocking, calling your name so he can see you turn your head and see him. Hear him. Like a child who hears his father's voice calling to him across the room, David turned right to him. "Yes, Daddy? Here I am." Can I ask you reader if that is your first impulse? I truly hope so. And if it isn't, it can become so. We have a friend in heaven and his door is open. Christ has opened it. Let's respond immediately. Let's speak when we hear him calling in life's burdens.

Familial Confidence

The third quality of David's prayer life was asking with a *familial confidence*. Consider again verses 9-10:

> *Hide not your face from me. Turn not your servant away in anger, O you who have been my help. Cast me not off; forsake me not, O God of my salvation! For my father and my mother have forsaken me, but the Lord will take me in.*

Asking not only with confidence, but with a *familial* confidence is the key to his request here. It is helpful to see that this is not the same as a *legal* confidence. It is not as if David is coming before the Lord as someone would approach an impersonal judge saying, "Your honor, I have a legal document here that states you must help me." A relationship between a judge and a local citizen is not based on love or family, but on legality. No, this is more than that. This is a familial confidence that boasts of all that being in God's family means.

When we approach God, we often are coming from a place of abandonment, of divorce, of brokenness of all kinds. Orphans with no family. This is how David felt--alone. He's concerned that even God himself could forsake him, and he pleads with God to not cast him aside or hide himself from David. As he thinks about what is going on in his life, we hear the mingling in his prayer of faith and fear, and it is as if David is saying, "God, don't forget about me. Don't forget about me. You've been my help in the past. Don't abandon me. Everyone else has." He's wrestling through hurt and pain and the fear of rejection like a lot of us have carried with us for years. But he finally proclaims, "...the Lord will take me in." This is the beginning of a familial confidence of faith. Many of us come from deep sin in our lives, from shattered homes and relationships. Can we begin to have this kind of confidence with God? We can. This type of confidence comes only from the gospel, only from Christ and our understanding of the implications of Christ's death, his atonement and resurrection. Follow me closely on this next statement. *Many of us have a tendency to constantly view ourselves through the lens of our own guilty conscience when we sin.* We wrestle with this every day. We rehearse to ourselves, almost as a constant backdrop of muttering: "Surely I'm not worthy of God's love. Surely I'm not worthy of God hearing my prayers. Surely I'm not worthy of God's help."

Read carefully. *Well, of course we're not!* We're absolutely not worthy! That's not why God is going to accept our prayers and open the door...because he finally finds us worthy. You know that already, looking at yourself. Let me be frank, dear reader, and state that you'll find a thousand reasons for God not to receive you in and of yourself. And do you know what that does? It only adds to your fear and anxieties. It doesn't take them away. Sometimes this sense of unworthiness doesn't come from an overwhelming, crippling shame over our sinfulness, but from a past experience of abandonment or rejection. For some of us it's both. David feels this abandonment as he literally says, "...my father and my mother have forsaken me." The word forsaken literally means *abandoned*. Betrayed. Bereft. Divorced. Some people view themselves all their life through this lens. "I don't belong. I'm an outcast. Nobody loves me." They say that being forsaken by family can be one of the deepest sorrows in life. I've not experienced that specifically but I know some of you have, and for some it is a lifetime of trying to overcome that.

We have no record of David literally being forsaken by his mother and father in his life. That hasn't been written in Scripture. But as the young anointed king, David was quickly forced to leave the protective umbrella of his family name and his household. And by the time he was a mature man growing up, his parents were long gone. He faced what God called him to face as the chosen ruler without the support and help of his parents. Undoubtedly, David probably often felt at times as if his parents had abandoned him because he followed God's path for him without their help. He felt like a deserted child and troubles have a way of highlighting that.

Troubles have a way of accentuating what is in your heart. If you have any sense that you don't belong, you're an outcast, you're an outsider, you don't fit in with anybody, you're not accepted, you're alone--trials have a way of heightening this sense of desertion, and fear begins to isolate you all the more. If you identify yourself in this manner, this is only going to add to your turmoil. David breaks through this with the relieving, comforting truth that the Lord will "take him in"! The Lord will bring David into his household. And under the cross of Jesus Christ, the Lord has taken you in. You belong to him and he's taking you in with a much further understanding of the depth of his relational love to you than he took in David who approached God through the Old Testament ordinances. The covenant name of God in the Old Testament was Yahweh, the great I AM. The covenant name of God to us in the New Covenant is, wonderfully and tenderly, Abba, which means *Daddy or Father*. Father?? That was virtually unknown to the Jews under the Old Covenant. This is how far God has brought you into his love and care and mercy. Jesus taught us to pray by first saying "Our Father who art in heaven..." (Matt 6:9).

He is our Father now, which means he has brought you into a family and not just into a new legal status. Praise God for his justification of you and the removal of your sins, but praise him all the more for not only acquitting you, but stepping down from the judgment throne and wrapping you in his arms of adoptive love.

Having familial confidence to approach God in this way finds its roots in being brought into a family forever and having the privilege of being a son of God. Read the following verses from Galatians 4:4-5: "But when the fullness of time had come, God sent forth his Son, born of woman, born under the law, to redeem those who were under the law, so that we might receive adoption as sons." It is important to see the word *sons* here and not just *children* because both are used in the New Testament. At the time that Paul the apostle wrote this, he was living under the rule of the Roman Empire, of which he was a citizen. According to Roman custom, it was specifically sons who were adopted by childless men or women (usually later in life, not as infants), to receive the inheritance and all the privileges and the rights of that Roman citizenship.

Paul declares that we are all, male and female, sons of God (not that women become men but the term *sons* is used representative of both men and women as equal inheritors of God's familial love). He sent his Son into the world that we might receive adoption *as* sons. And he explains that because we are sons now, God sent the Spirit of his Son into our hearts crying, *Abba, Father.* Like orphans arriving home for the very first time, marvel at the depth of the love you now have been lavished upon by God. Picture a Roman servant leading a young man into the polished, stately courtyard of his adoptive parents' home, and all that he sees now belongs to him. This is his home forever. Envision the father and mother, anticipating his arrival, flinging open the double doors at the top of the stone stairs, and descending purposefully towards him, arms open wide, eager desire in their eyes to welcome him, to bring him in, to love and dote upon him. This is God's love for you. I John 3:1 says, "See what kind of love the Father has given to us, that we should be called children of God; and so we are." We are his children. We're sons of God. "But to all who did receive him, who believed in his name, he gave the right to become children of God" (John1:12). He loves us deeply. Don't wait outside but come in, calling upon his name with all the confidence of a son.

Jesus's instruction to pray to God as "Our Father who Art in heaven…" has really touched me as I meditate upon all this. It has really taken my prayer life to a deeper level of talking to God like my Father because I know what it is to be an earthly father myself. And I know that he is the perfect Father and that where I've failed as one, he will never fail. What comfort and healing there is in this truth! I remember Charles Spurgeon's testimony of his wrestling with God in prayer during one of the times when he was intensely suffering from the pain of gout.

> *When I was racked some months ago with pain, to an extreme degree, so that I could no longer bear it without crying out, I asked all to go from the room, and leave me alone; and then I had nothing I could say to God but this, 'Thou art my Father, and I am thy child; and thou, as a Father, art tender and full of mercy. I could not bear to see my child suffer as thou makest me suffer, and if I saw him tormented as I am now, I would do what I could to help him, and put my arms under him to sustain him. Wilt thou hide thy face from me, my Father? Wilt thou still lay on a heavy hand, and not give me a smile from thy countenance?' . . . so I pleaded, and I ventured to say, when I was quiet, and they came back who watched me: 'I shall never have such pain again from this*

moment, for God has heard my prayer.' I
bless God that ease came and the racking pain never
returned.[29]

May our prayers rise to that level of familial confidence
with God.

Allow me to illustrate further our Heavenly Father's
delight in receiving us as his children. If one of my
grandchildren (and they've done this) comes into my room
at 3a.m. when he spends the night and he says, "Papi
(pronounced "Poppy"), I'm thirsty," what am I going to do?
Roll over and snuggle deeper into the covers? No, I'm going
to get up and fill him a glass of cool water. But if a complete
stranger came into my bedroom at 3a.m., I'd say, "Who are
you and what are you doing here? What are you coming here
for?" Not so with my grandchildren. That's the kind of access
we have and we should, like my little ones, boldly enter into
God's chambers. I think what happens at times is we forget
the depth of the implications of adoption. In his classic
volume, "Knowing God", J.I. Packer ventures to propose
that adoption may be a higher privilege even than
justification. He explains,

> *Adoption is a family idea, conceived in terms of love,*
> *and viewing God as father. In adoption, God takes*
> *us into his family and fellowship—he establishes us*
> *as his children and heirs. Closeness, affection and*
> *generosity are at the heart of the relationship. To be*
> *right with God the Judge is a great thing, but to be*
> *loved and cared for by God the Father is a greater*
> (thing).[30]*

Though justification is foundational to the gospel and the

---

[29] Dr. Darrel W. Amundsen, The Anguish and Agonies of Charles Spurgeon,
Christian History Magazine Issue #29, 1991.
[30] J. I. Packer, *Knowing God,* (Downers Grove, Illinois: IVP, 1973), 207.

church does indeed stand or fall fully upon that doctrine, adoption might be a greater blessing. We've not only been acquitted, we've been brought into a family. I think what we sometimes need in order to pray with this sort of urgency and a sense of familial confidence is to talk to our God as if with our dad—to harbor no misgivings about how it sounds as we blurt it out, or how confused we sound, or how rambling it becomes. Truly he understands it all. When we explain our problems to the Lord, including all the messy details and our reactions like "then he said and then I said" and "I yelled at my wife today but I'm still not sorry and I know it's wrong" and "I went to the appointment but I'm afraid you're going to give me cancer, God"—when we speak like this to the Lord, we are pleading to his fatherhood like Spurgeon did. Share. Confess. Ask. Describe. We need to be taken deeper into our experience of God's Fatherhood in our life. And when I think of that, I think of D. Martin Lloyd Jones.

In his book, "Joy Unspeakable", Jones draws upon the writings of the puritan Thomas Goodwin and describes what I am referring to as a deeper experience of the Fatherhood of God. Jones writes:

> *A man and his little child (are) walking down the road and they are walking hand in hand, and the child knows that he is the child of his father, and he knows that his father loves him, and he rejoices in that, and he is happy in it. There is no uncertainty about it all, but suddenly the father, moved by some impulse, takes hold of the child and picks him up, fondles him in his arms, kisses him, embraces him, showers his love upon him, and then he puts him down again and they go on walking together.*
>
> *That is it! The child knew before that his father loved him, and he knew that he was his child. But oh! the loving embrace, this extra outpouring of love, this*

unusual manifestation of it — that is the kind of thing. The Spirit bearing witness with our spirit that we are the children of God.[31]

I think we cherish the fatherhood of God and adoption when we have experiences like that child's walk in this life. You may be thinking, "that's so subjective." But what is objective is the doctrine of adoption in Christ. It's importance in addressing anxiety is made clear by John Stott:

A Christian's freedom from anxiety is not due to some guaranteed freedom from trouble, but to the folly of worry and especially to the confidence that God is our Father, that even permitted suffering is within the orbit of His care.[32]

And if you have never experienced anything like this degree of affirmation, it may be you need to dwell upon the objective truth of your adoption in Christ. Go to the Word and reflect upon adoption. Then you will begin to cherish it.

Now if you are fretting, or despairing, "I simply can't pray like this. I don't feel like that is my relationship with God," remember that sonship is something given--bequeathed. That's what the apostle John draws our attention to when he writes: "See what kind of love the Father has *given* to us..." (1 Jn. 3:1). It is something bestowed. You either are an adopted son or you're not. It is not about trying or attempting to become a child of God. It is impossible to make yourself God's child or be 50% adopted. There is no such thing. You have either *been adopted* by someone or you have not; you either are his child or you are not. It is not something you gain or achieve; it is a gracious gift that is granted to you.

---

[31] Martin Lloyd-Jones, *Joy Unspeakable*, (Wheaton, Illinois: Harold Shaw Publishers, 1985), 84.
[32] John Stott, *The Message of the Sermon on the Mount*, (Downers Grove: IVP, 1978), 167-168.

Today if you find you are unable to pray like this, either you need to relish again the reality of your adoption, going back and marveling once more at your access into God's courts as his child...or you may need to receive this gift of adoption for the very first time. And we receive Christ through faith and repentance. John states, "...as many as received Him, to them He gave the right to become children of God," (John 1:12). You can say, "Jesus, I receive you as my Lord and Savior." I hope that is true of you, and if it is, let's relish it! Cherish the fact that we can talk to the Creator of the universe. Think of the magnitude of his mind and his power, and that we know him as our Father in heaven. When our lives are full of fear and our troubles vex our souls, like David, let's pray with earnest impudence. Let's pray with a responsive immediacy. But above all this, let's pray with a childlike familial confidence. Our Father loves us.

"Humble yourselves, therefore, under the mighty hand of God...casting all your anxieties on him, because he cares for you"
1 Peter 5:6-7.

Whom Shall I Fear?

4

FOLLOWING

Teach me your way, O Lord, and lead me on a level path because of my enemies. Give me not up to the will of my adversaries; for false witnesses have risen against me, and they breathe out violence.
Psalm 27:11

Psalm 27 gifts us with David's strategy for overcoming fear and anxiety, and we have noted that there are five different components to this transforming process. The first is **trusting** in God's protective love (verses 1-3). Secondly, he tells us to be **seeking** God's presence as the highest priority in our lives (verses 4-6). Thirdly we ought to be **asking** for God's aid urgently and boldly, responding swiftly to his call to us to draw near to him when we are afraid (verses 7-10). The clearest insight we have into what David was experiencing when he wrote the psalm brings us to the fourth component: **following** God's ways. David states in verse 12, "false witnesses have risen against me and they breathe out violence." Enduring such false accusations and hatred towards him caused David to cry out passionately to the Lord, crying "lead me" (verse 11), and "teach me your way, O Lord, and lead me on a level path."

Walking by faith in this way, fellow Christians, is rewarded with a peace from God during fearful times. Overcoming our fears, then, encompasses not just *trusting*, *seeking* and *asking*, but embraces obedience and submission in *following* where he leads, though the path may be difficult. I admit it is easy to succumb to a temporary fix or a sinful response when fears are overwhelming our emotions and our mental or psychological state. Yet, we learn from David here that rather than crumbling with fear, compromising our integrity, or trying to resolve the situation out of our own flesh and reasoning, we need to ask God to teach us. Times when fears arise are times that should lead us to say, "Lord, teach me." But can we with integrity ask God for deliverance if we are not willing to walk in his ways? In fact, doing what is right may finally prove the way out of or through the hardship. And not only that, (and what this chapter will be explaining), obeying the Lord in the midst of our adversities will ultimately bring the peace we desire, and bring us closer to him.

This concept is found especially in the neighboring Psalms 23 and 25. I have mentioned that our Psalm 27 has some themes that are found in a small grouping of the psalms beginning with Psalm 23, and all the way through Psalm 30. Psalm 23 says, "he leads me beside still waters. He leads me in paths of righteousness," and Psalm 25:4-5 says, "Make me to know your ways, O Lord, teach me your paths. Lead me in your truth and teach me." From Psalm 27:11 I hope to show you the connection between obedience, following God's ways, and overcoming fear. We will also refer heavily to Psalm 25 because of its relationship with Psalm 27. We have two questions to answer as we look at verse 11: what is involved in following God's ways? And how does this help in overcoming fears?

What Is Involved in Following God's Ways?

The simple one-word answer to what is involved in following God's ways is obedience, but what underlies obedience? From Psalm 27 and Psalm 25 there are three things that underlie obedience: a *teachable spirit*, a *submissive heart*, and a *reverential fear*.

Teachable spirit

In verse 11, David says, "Teach me your way." Oh, for a classroom of students who chime, "Teach us!" when the teacher walks into the room. That is a teachable spirit and we need one if we are to follow him. You can hear a heart that says, "I want to learn." Here is a reminder that the Christian life is about learning. Our whole walk with Christ is about learning. It's about growing. Woe to those who come to that place in the Christian walk where they think they have arrived at the mastery of all knowledge and perfection, especially those who teach with that attitude. I tell you there is no such thing until we are taken up in glory, and it should be a mark of every congregation of believers, and a mark of our lives as brothers and sisters in Christ, that we remain teachable. Always covet the desire to learn. When David says, "teach me your way," he is not referring to a set of specific directions, like teach me what school to attend, or teach me what job to take. He is speaking here about moral principles; what is your moral will right now, dear God, in this situation that is causing me so much consternation, fear, and anxiety? Look at Psalm 25:4, "Make me to know your ways, (notice the plural there) O Lord, teach me your paths." Then, in verse 5, "Lead me in your truth." It is not a desire to come to some higher level of self-mastery, but to become a student of God in the school of life where he specifically is desiring you to grow.

In other words, ask yourself questions like these: At this time in my life, what should I really be thinking about?

Focusing my time and attention on? What fills my thoughts as my chief desire right now? How am I thinking wrongly or rightly about my life as God's child in this specific relationship, job or role? How should I conduct myself in this situation in a godly manner? What actions right now in my life would be in harmony with God's will? Which habits are not? What would glorify Christ most in this affliction that is overwhelming me and giving me so much distress? How can I react rightly here? This sort of reflective analysis prepares the soil of the heart for the work of the Master. Paul says in 1 Corinthians 10:31, "Whatever you do, do all to the glory of God." A teachable spirit that is ready for growth is what underlies all of the obedient actions that follow in conforming to God's ways.

As such we ought not to simply cry to God for deliverance, but for guidance and instruction, as David does. This is important because times of fear are times that God has sent into our lives to mature us, to change us, and to teach us. Do not let such an opportunity pass you by to be taught by the Great Teacher. Every temptation to fear is at the same time an opportunity to grow in your understanding of God in some way, and to increase in your faith as you ask him to guide you and instruct you. Even, and I would say especially, the times that we are in trouble or in fear because of our own foolish decisions or waywardness are times to learn by asking the question, "Where did I go wrong? How did I mess things up this time? Lord, teach me. Here I am again."

Then there may be other times when you did no wrong. In fact, you are in trouble because you did right. You were honest at work, and now you may lose your job. You spoke the truth, and now that relationship is gone. There will be times when you find yourself pressed into a corner because you did what was right. Perhaps you went out of your way to love someone and you involved yourself in another's cares or burdens, but all that did was bring you trouble, and you're beginning to feel oppressed. You're fearful of what might happen. This may be a time not to ask the Lord to teach you what you did wrong, but to teach you *through* this. In Psalm 119, which some have attributed to David, verse 71 says, "It is good for me that I was afflicted." Probably not the most popular quote to go on a mug or a tee shirt, right?[33] But yet it holds true. We don't like to acknowledge the fact that God often uses unpleasant experiences to teach us, but we would do well to accept this reality and change our perspective on the value of God's tool of affliction. There is immense value from it, though at times it does not feel that way. The rest of that verse reads, "that I might learn your statutes." He is acknowledging that there are some glorious things we just won't learn from books, but from sovereignly bestowed hardships, so it is beneficial for us to be afflicted that we might learn them.

Martin Luther, the great reformer, said, "I never knew the meaning of God's Word until I came into affliction." It seems like an overstatement, but he adds, "I have always found it one of my best school-masters."[34] How true. Reflecting on Psalm 119:71, Puritan Charles Bridges in his commentary says, "How can we have any experimental acquaintance with the promises of God except under those circumstances for which the promises are made?"[35] Hear what he's saying, O Christian. You will never know what a promise means unless you find yourself in a situation for which the promise was given. Consider a generic promise like Psalm 50:15, which Charles Spurgeon famously called the

---

[33] When I preached this psalm and emphasized this point, the following week I found a mug on my desk with that very inscription. It was made and given by a member of our congregation. It sits on my shelf to this day.

[34] Quoted in Charles Bridges, *An Exposition of Psalm 119* (Edinburgh: Banner of Truth, Reprinted 1987), 182.

[35] Charles Bridges, *An Exposition of Psalm 119* (Edinburgh: Banner of Truth, Reprinted 1987), 182.

Robinson Crusoe verse: "[You] will call on me in the day of trouble. I will deliver you and you shall glorify me."

How will you ever know that promise to be true unless you have a day of trouble, and what you finally then do is call upon the Lord, and then he *does* deliver you, and then you *do* praise him? A crisis moment like that, full of trembling, is a time to have a teachable spirit. If we desire to walk in his ways--to follow Christ, we must have that teachable spirit. In Hebrews 5:8, we are told that the Son of God, though he was a son, yet learned obedience from the things which he suffered. This is showing us that even Jesus, God's Son had to experience the breadth of human suffering according to the will of the Father. Should we expect less for ourselves? As we learned in our last chapter, we are God's sons and he is our Father in his adoption of us. He will, therefore, never fail to teach us as a wise and loving Father ought to. We are always children in God's school.

Are you willing to listen? Are you willing to consider and ask questions like, "Tell me, Lord, what did I do wrong? What can I do differently? If I did right, then, how can I get through this? Secondly, are you willing to change? Do you want to change? Because that's why these things are brought into our lives at times... to conform us to the image of his Son.

Submissive heart

To follow God's ways also necessitates a submissive heart. David says, "Teach me your way, Oh Lord, and lead me on a level path." The desire to be led implies a willingness to follow. We can ask the Lord to teach us, but we may not follow. However, if we ask to be led, it is implied we *want* to follow, that we will take the Lord's instructions and go with Him. It is as if David is saying, "I don't want to intellectually understand how I ought to think rightly to overcome my fears and then just remain there. I want you to lead me forward because *I intend to follow.*" This is more than knowledge. David specifically asks God to lead him on "the level path" because of his enemies and the people who are breathing out violence against him. What does he mean by the level path? Some think he is implying a path free of obstacles, and safe from his enemies. But Hebrew parallelism (the fact that Scripture balances concepts from one scripture with coordinating other scripture) and the context of the other surrounding psalms imply that this is not a path free of pain or adversaries, but "a righteous path". This parallels his saying, "teach me your way," which refers to moral principles--doing the right thing. At this time, David is requesting God to lead him in that righteous path so that he may not fall into temptation. Likewise, in Psalm 23, he says, God "leads me in the paths of righteousness." This is his desire. He wants to be led in the paths of righteousness by God. For us, to receive Christ as our Savior and Lord is to receive him not only as the one who is the means of our justification and forgiveness, but as our guide: "If anyone would come after me, let him deny himself and take up his cross daily and follow me" (Luke 9:23).

To follow me, says Jesus, is to know him as Lord and Savior, and to know him as our model and leader. In 1 John 2:6, John says, "whoever says he abides in him ought to walk in the same way in which he walked," and the word *walk* there means to *live*—to live in the same way as Jesus lived. Paul could even say in 1 Corinthians 11:1, "Be imitators of me, as I am of Christ." Paul models a life of obedience in imitating Christ. Growing as God's pupils involves more than just getting head knowledge. It involves following—putting into practice in imitation of the Master--and that may be the hardest part. I think it is easier to collect knowledge. It is far harder to put that knowledge into practice. It is easy to read books on marriage (and we have a glut of them), but it is another thing to live out godly characteristics with your spouse. It is easy to read books on parenting, and quite another thing to actively and lovingly raise your own children in the grace and discipline of the Lord. This is what David is acknowledging, like so many of us ought to, that he desperately *needs* to be taught by the Lord at this time of his life. He wants God to not only tell him, but to show him, and to pull him along on this righteous path. In like manner, we also should commit ourselves to asking God to lead us so that we can grow in applying what he has taught us at this stage of our lives.

We see, then, that distressing trials are a time to be *taught* AND a time to be *led*—and we *follow*. It involves a teachable spirit and involves, secondly, a submissive heart, a heart that says, "Lead me. I'm ready to follow," and this is especially important because the difficult seasons are when you can easily be taken captive. At the arrest of Jesus, Peter was tempted to fear man and the moment he was overcome by that (perhaps he feared the people around him, or physical suffering, or ostracization), he fell into temptation. He denied the Lord three times. The same may happen to us. It is a time to pause in our hearts, not rushing into any decisions, but to humbly pray, "Lord, what should I do? Walk with me in that righteous path right now. Lord, I'm so overwhelmed by emotion. I'm afraid I'm going to make a foolish decision. Help me, guide me, and search my heart."

A great prayer at this time would be from Psalm 139, again from David, where in the well-known verse at the end of the psalm, David prays, "Search me, O God and know my heart. Try me and know my thoughts and see if there be any grievous way in me and lead me..." Show me my wrong thinking. Show me the passions that are ruling my life, and then lead me "...in the way everlasting."

Reverential fear

There is a third element involved in following God's way. There is also, and perhaps most fundamentally so, a sense of reverential fear within our relationship with God. It is not stated explicitly in Psalm 27, but it is in the nearby psalm, Psalm 25, which contains similar themes. Verse 4 states, "make me to know your ways," just as in verse 11 of Psalm 27, where he says, "teach me your paths. Lead me in your truth." But then notice this connection in verse 12 of Psalm 25: "who is the man who fears the Lord? Him will he instruct in the way that he should choose." Who is God going to lead and teach? "Him who fears the Lord." Girding up both learning and following lies the foundational principle of fearing the Lord.

This implies that a submissive spirit and a teachable heart are things that one has because one has already cultivated a reverential fear. They are pillars built upon it, with the fear of the Lord being the foundation. Scripture teaches that if you have a teachable spirit, you will be gaining wisdom. But Scripture also tells us that the *fear of the Lord* is the beginning of wisdom! We can see from this passage that the cornerstone of learning and following is the fearing of him, and that is the bedrock upon which we build to have a teachable spirit and a submissive heart. This is how we mature in faith.

What does it mean to fear the Lord? If you were to look it up in a Hebrew lexicon, you would find that the word *fear* itself literally means "to be terrified, to cower, and to tremble", and in many contexts, that's exactly what it should mean. But within the framework of a covenant relationship, which we as Christians have, the fear of the Lord refers primarily to the fact that we revere him, and we respect him. We hold him in the highest regard with both awe and adoring love. We don't cower at his feet because we fear his condemnation, even though we respect mightily his sovereign power. As our Heavenly Father he can discipline us just like an earthly father disciplines his son. But in this sacred bond of a covenantal relationship, there is no fear of banishment or wrathful punishment as payment for our sins. That punishment has been exhausted upon his Son Jesus on our behalf. Within the context of our sonship, we revere God because he alone has saved, and redeemed us. While holding every right and all power and authority to condemn us to hell, he has forgiven us. Thus, we cherish and esteem him. We recognize his awesomeness and the depth of his grace and mercy towards us. The fear of the Lord, really, is a quality that I would say is not merely essential to living the Christian life but one that without, one cannot be a Christian.

I want to contemplate this bond of reverential fear within the New Covenant further because it is so powerful to encourage us. Jeremiah 31 is one of the key places in the Old Testament where the New Covenant is promised for the future. Within this covenant is a promise that God will give his people a new heart. Speaking through the prophet, the Lord promises, "Behold, the days are coming, declares the Lord, when I will make a new covenant with the house of Israel and the house of Judah." Later, in chapter 32 he expands upon the promises of the New Covenant stating,

> …*they shall be my people, and I will be their God. I will give them one heart and one way, that they may fear me forever, for their own good and the good of their children after them. I will make with them an everlasting covenant, that I will not turn away from doing good to them. And I will put the fear of me in their hearts, that they may not turn from me. (Jer. 32:38-40)*

Notice that last phrase, "I will put the fear of me in their hearts." There we see the promise of the transformation of a sinner's heart. Sinners like us. In other places he speaks about this same new heart as a circumcised heart, and in all these instances God is talking about the same thing—the miracle of regeneration, of being born again.

It is true that the prophet is talking contextually of the promised nation, who many times turned away from the Lord. But we learn from the book of Romans in the New Testament that gentiles have been grafted into this very promise that he first gave and revealed to the Israelites (Rom. 11:11-24). This promise is ours too! If you are a Christian today, he has given you a new heart of love and devotion to him, and you know it is a miracle. Because God loved you, he called you and gave you life. In a very real sense, he graciously deposited the fear of himself in you because you had none. Before his intervention in your soul, you did not fear God or perhaps did not even believe he existed. Even if you were convinced of his generic existence, you had no respect for him. You didn't bow the knee to him. There was no repentance. You didn't take God or his word seriously; his laws and his commandments seriously. You didn't see him as the source of life everlasting. When God says he put the fear of himself in you, he filled your new heart with reverential respect and love for him.

In Romans 3:18, Paul says of unbelievers, "There is no fear of God before their eyes." If today you have yet to fear the Lord in your heart, allow me to briefly address you. I can tell you with great sadness and trepidation for you that someday you will fear him. There will be no escaping it. It will be on the day of condemnation. Though many think such a statement unloving, I think it loving to warn you by speaking to you frankly as the Lord himself does. What you mock now will one day be clearly revealed as the truth and your fear of God then on that final day of judgment will be limited to a cowering, trembling, terrifying experience of knowing that he who knows all about you has exposed your heart; and you stand condemned before him. I pray with all my heart that you will not experience that kind of fear but will turn to him right now and place your faith in God and his Son. Jesus says, "Truly, truly, I say to you, whoever hears my word and believes him who sent me has eternal life. He does not come into judgment, but has passed from death to life" (John 5:24).

I must now stress that we who know the Lord have a fear of the Lord that is not servile. It is not a cowering nor slave-like fear. It is a filial, humble, and reverential fear, full of love, and the difference is the transformation we have experienced through the gospel. We have experienced the grace of God, have known the grace of God, and we thankfully rejoice that we are safe because of it. We have "passed from death to life!" Dr. Burk Parsons says, "The gospel is the difference between being afraid of God and fearing God."[36] If you are a Christian, you fear the Lord in this right sense, and you ought not to be afraid of God's condemnation. As Puritan John Flavel observed, "Godly fear does not arise from a perception of God as hazardous, but glorious."[37]

Let this truth sink deeply into your heart so that you can follow and submit to him all the more with joyful awe for his saving love.

How Is Following Helpful to Overcoming Anxiety?

How is all of this helpful to overcoming fears and anxieties? How does obedience rooted in the fear of the Lord overcome the fears that tie your stomach in knots? I've actually read several times that the number one fear, even greater than death, is the fear of public speaking. How does obedience in following the Lord help you overcome whatever those things are that make you fret and tremble in your soul each day?

---

[36] Dr. Burk Parsons, "The Fear of the Lord", *Tabletalk Magazine*, January 2018.
[37] Matt Smethurst, "What Are We Afraid Of?", *Tabletalk Magazine*, January 2018.

From the Old Testament

Here is a key: The fear of the Lord brings an experiential intimacy with God that is absolutely essential in times of crisis. Look back at Psalm 25, which, as we have noted, echoes the same themes that are found in verse 11 of Psalm 27. Verse 12 states, "Who is the man who fears the Lord? Him will He instruct in the way that he should choose. His soul shall abide in well-being." The ideal God-fearer is our Lord Jesus. His soul knew the well-being of the presence of the Father throughout his sufferings. But this much of the verse applies also to you and me as well, for it follows "and his offspring shall inherit the land." This referred to the land of Canaan intended by God for the Jews, but ultimately, the whole earth will be the Kingdom of God and believers in Christ will possess it (Matt. 5:5; Rev. 11:15). Lastly, the next verse (Psalm 25:14) is the one to meditate and savor as we consider our comforting intimacy with Christ in fearing him today: "The friendship of the Lord is for those who fear him, and he makes known to them his covenant."

The friendship of God belongs to those who fear him. This is astounding! The word "friendship" in the ESV is a tricky little word. The New American Standard and the New King James translate it as "secret." This might sound like two different things, and interestingly, the New International Version provides yet a third translation by translating it with a verb, "confides" in the Lord. But according to the "Theological Wordbook of the Old Testament", a key Hebrew Lexicon, the primary meaning of the word is "confidential speech."[38] This implies more intimate counsel than general advice. It is the kind of confidential speech given

---

[38] R. Laird Harris, Gleason L. Archer Jr., and Bruce K. Waltke, eds., *Theological Wordbook of the Old Testament* (Chicago: Moody Press, 1999), 619.

to a circle of trusted friends. There is an intimacy being described here that belongs only to those who fear the Lord, those to whom God, as someone once put it, "gives whispers from heaven, as it were."

He speaks to them. He guides them. God is the close and communicative friend of those who obey.

Abraham immediately comes to mind for he was called the friend of God. And when God sent the Angel of the Lord, likely a preincarnate visit of Christ, to judge Sodom and to bring Lot out, he first came to Abraham, and said, "Shall I hide from Abraham what I'm about to do?" (Genesis 18:17). No, he would not keep it secret. He would tell him, because Abraham was a friend of the Lord, and God opened up his heart to Abraham and the plans of his mind intended for Sodom. And that is the kind of relationship that we need when our hearts are full of fear and anxiety arising from crisis situations in our lives. If our heart is set to fear and obey the Lord, this is what we will receive. A responsive, loving Friend who will communicate his counsel, his love and friendship, and his personal response to the struggles we have described to him in prayer. Today, God speaks personally and directly to us through his written word by the Holy Spirit. Consider again Psalm 25:12: "Him will He instruct in the way that he should choose."

Consider also what David affirms in the latter part of Psalm 24:14, "he makes known to them his covenant." By this, he means that, like a friend speaking to you, he will remind *you* of his promised and securing love toward *you* and bring into your experiential knowledge, the blessings of the covenant. It will be a time when God speaks to you mightily. I can attest that in times of crisis in my life I have wrestled mightily with thinking that I don't want to be anxious, but yet I still was. I knew I shouldn't be anxious, but I couldn't stop, and the conflict of my desires (to trust the Lord or be anxious) was killing me. It was tying me all up in knots. Every time I would wake up in the middle of the night, the first thing I would think about was the situation or person I was anxious over but then my conscience butted in, telling me I shouldn't be worried about this. It can feel like a tiring, around-the-clock battle for domination of your mind's thoughts, and a continual loop of worry, confession, repentance, restoration, and back to worrying. That's when you want God pressing the promises of his covenant deeper into your heart, reminding you of his love, reminding you of a steadfast faithfulness, reminding you that his mercies are new day after day. We want the Spirit to help us recall, "And behold, I am with you always to the end of the age" (Matt. 28:20). This is the experiential intimacy of which I am speaking.

This is not to say that God will give you deeper insight than is available to all believers. The notion of "whispers from heaven" does not, in my estimation, mean private, little, audible voices instructing, "Turn left here. Buy this or sell that." Rather, he speaks to us through the truth that he has given us, driving home its application to our situation. You will be convinced this is the truth that applies right now in your circumstance, revealed clearly to you *as if* God did whisper it from heaven. This is the mind-illuminating, heart-warming and convicting ministry of the Holy Spirit. Again, it is not some *new* revelation that he has not imparted to anyone else. But when he does speak to you through the word and his Spirit, impressing upon your mind the principles and promises that will aid you, do not delay in trusting him. You need to hear this voice louder than you are hearing the voices of the things that are threatening you, and troubling you, and giving you all this angst. God is your friend (if you indeed love and fear him) who will tell you the blessings of his covenant, that you may know he is with you. When you experience this intimacy with God, you will know you have it, and this will help you to make any decisions that were distressing to you, and you can walk once more in the confidence of the Lord. You can say, "I've done my part. I made the right choice. Everything else is really God's." You can say, as David says in Psalm 23, "Even though I walk through the valley of the shadow of death, I will fear no evil, because you are with me." We have this friendship with God through Christ every moment of every day. Are we listening?

In summary, God is not just some sort of nebulous power or vague force. He is your heavenly friend! Isaiah 41:10 confidently affirms, "Fear not for I am with you." The one who knows God is with him is that person who fears the Lord, who has a humble and submissive heart, a teachable spirit, a reverential respect for God, and who wants to walk in his ways. And he goes on, "...be not dismayed, for I am your God; I will strengthen you, I will help you, I will uphold you with my righteous, right hand." Again, those who have this confidence are those who fear the Lord. But let us go beyond seeing our friendship with God through the Old Testament promises to the patriarchs of Israel, David's Old Covenant experience. Imagine this, we now hear that whisper from heaven with a clearer, greater, and more profound depth than David ever knew!

By the time we come to the Gospel of Jesus Christ in the New Covenant to which we belong today, the whispers from heaven become more like bellowed declarations shouted from the rooftops! In the New Covenant we learn that our friendship with Christ has given us insight into everything that God is doing and all of his purposes. We understand what life is about much more fully. We've been told in Ephesians 1 that God is working all things according to the counsel of his will. We are told that we are the Church, and that Jew and Gentile alike have been brought into one temple, and God is building that temple. It is the dwelling place of God through his Spirit into which he is bringing his elect from all the nations (Eph. 2:21). We are told that God is causing all things to work together for good to those who love God, to those who are called according to his purpose (Rom. 8:28). We are given insight into the fact that all of this is conforming us into the image of his Son. We know that the Son is coming back, that his kingdom is going to be fully established. These are more than whispers from heaven; they are proclamations from heaven. Fear not. Think big. Realize the greatness of which you are a part. This is your life story. Let's consider some explicit examples now from the lips of Jesus.

From the New Testament

Luke 12:32 states "fear not little flock..." I love that verse. What do you think these big, burly fishermen thought when he said that to them? "...fear not, for it is your Father's good pleasure to give you the kingdom." Jesus is saying, "You're never going to earn it. You're not going to merit it. Fear not that your sin will keep you out of the kingdom, for I have come to take your sins away, and God desires to give you all that you need for this life, and he will give you the kingdom to come. You have nothing to fear now about this life or the next." If you've placed your faith in Christ, do not fear that whatever is happening in life is going to cause you to lose out. Fear not, little flock, for your Father delights in giving you the kingdom of God, that precious jewel, the pearl above all others. It is God's pleasure to give it to you. What a statement!

When Jesus said such things to the disciples, he was teaching them why they could become radically generous and invest themselves in kingdom work. He was telling them why they could give their possessions away freely without fear; for, whatever they would lose, and however generous they might be, God had given them the kingdom. The kingdom to come, the new creation, the new heavens and new earth, it all belonged to them, and it belongs to us too. There is a way the kingdom is present right now, what some call "*the already*", and then there is a future consummation of the kingdom or "*the not yet.*" To say that the kingdom of God has been given to us now is to say that, right now, the reason we can change, or be radically generous, and spiritually grow is because the power of the kingdom to reorient our life has already broken into our lives. It has invaded our very souls. We are enabled to reorient our passions and our hearts. God has already given us the good news of the gospel, and we have the power to live according to Christ's word. Fear not where obedience might take you, because you are doing what is right in going where God has led, and in doing what God has taught you. Fear not the consequences that might come from the world while we still live in a fallen world. Fear not, for God has already given you the kingdom. Though in one sense we may be poor, we are, in another sense, as Paul says, the richest people in the world (1 Cor. 3:21).

Consider yet another example from Matthew 10:31, where Christ says, "Fear not, for you are of more value than many sparrows." He goes on to ask the disciples, if God is concerned and connected to the needs of one little sparrow, is he going to overlook you? Will he say, "Oops, I forgot about you there in your little church." No, fear not; he most surely knows your circumstances. I find it astounding, and you might find it interesting that the most repeated command in the Bible is actually, "Fear not" (70 times in the NIV not including other variations).

Lastly, Jesus assures his followers, "In the world you will have tribulation. But take heart; I have overcome the world." (John 16:33.) Yes, we can expect a lot of trouble in this fallen world. You and I have been redeemed from the guilt of sin, but we have not been set free entirely from the presence and pollution of sin. Therefore, in this life we will have tribulation, but we need not fear, because God has overcome it. In John 16, Jesus was giving them the promise of the Helper, who is the Holy Spirit. God helps you and me to overcome the things that are troubling our lives by having given us his Spirit. Fear not, because the Spirit dwells in you. Christ has overcome the world. He will guide you and enable you to navigate through life's circumstances and whatever happens as a result of doing what is right. "Do not be frightened, and do not be dismayed" (Joshua 1:9), for he has already given you the kingdom, and you have all things in Christ.

Concluding Reflections

When we fear the Lord, we need not fear anyone else. Isaiah, speaking to the nation that was trembling due to rumors of what might be coming down upon them at the hands of another nation, said, "...do not fear what they fear, nor be in dread. But the Lord of hosts, him you shall honor as holy. Let him be your fear, and let him be your dread. And he will become a sanctuary..." (Isaiah 8:12-14). Let the Lord be the one whom you fear. And when you do, he will become a sanctuary to you. You will not need to fear anyone or anything else. His friendship, his plans, his purposes, his comfort, and his presence will all be made known to you, not merely intellectually, but through an inward sense of conviction. This is yet again what Paul calls the "peace of God which surpasses all understanding," that guards our hearts in Christ Jesus. (Phil. 4:7).

So, whatever it is that you fear, my friends, or that you fear may come, whatever ties your stomach in knots, remember, there is a *right fear* and there is a *wrong fear*. A stomach that remains tied in knots is the wrong fear. The right fear is the fear of the Lord. And if you have plenty of that awesome respect for the glory of God, it casts out all the wrong fears. It will subdue them over time. God will show you what to do. He will lead you in his way. And this obedience rooted in the fear of the Lord will soothe your heart. It will make darkness into day. It will bring the friendship of God into focus when you need it most. "Praise the Lord! Blessed is the man who fears the Lord" (Psalm

112:1). Joy will come as you humbly follow the Lord with a teachable heart and a submissive spirit rising from the fear of the Lord. The Lord is our Shepherd. He wants to lead you to green pastures. He wants to bring you to rest beside quiet waters. Are you desiring to follow?

5

WAITING

I believe that I shall look upon the goodness of the Lord in the land of the living! Wait for the Lord; be strong, and let your heart take courage; wait for the Lord!
Psalm 27:13-14

Now, I have to confess right up front that there's a trend in my life that I'm not proud of, I hate waiting. I hate getting stuck in traffic. I don't like pausing for my internet or phone service to catch up while it downloads files. I dread long lines at the store. I always flit my eyes to and fro amongst the snaking trails of grocery carts like a hawk to find the shortest one at Costco. I don't like waiting for something that I think I need right away, because Amazon has now trained me that I can have almost anything I want within two days, and if I'm willing to pay a premium, maybe even one day. In fact, right now the company is working on being able to deliver an item within an hour by a drone which will fly to my yard and drop my package off. I admit I am both skeptical and somewhat delighted about it.

Yes, I admit it—waiting is not one of my favorite things

to do. That's the world you and I live in, isn't it? We live in an instantaneous society. Let's face it, we are becoming alarmingly comfortable with not having to wait, but, even with all our modern inventions and contraptions, waiting is still an unavoidable reality. You can still find pockets of it woven into the fabric of our lives. It is knitted into the creation. We have to wait for the rains, for the seasons. We may need snow in the mountains for our California water supply right now, but we must wait for the storms to roll through. The Christian life is also largely about waiting. We are waiting for the resurrection. We are waiting for the Second Coming. We hope and wait for the Lord. Waiting is part of this fallen world, and part of living in this present stage of the new creation (2 Cor. 5:17).

Individually, all of us are more than likely anticipating something, whether we are thoughtful of it at this moment or not. It may be that we are looking towards something anxiously that we desire; we may need a new career or a home to rent, and we are waiting for the phone call for an interview or a home rental ad to pop up. Some of us are waiting for a relationship; we would like to have Mr. Right or Mrs. Right, but perhaps he or she hasn't shown up yet, so we wait another year, or yet another ten years. I know there are many of us waiting upon one of the most personal and powerful yearnings as a Christian parent-- for the gift of faith to be bestowed to our children. We know that we cannot create or schedule that faith onto a calendar. It is in the hands of God, so we are compelled to wait. We just keep praying. Some of us dearly wait for physical healing for ourselves or for our loved ones.

We come now to the final study of David's strategy against his fears. As the last arrow in his quiver, David models how waiting *with hope* is his final weapon to wield in his battles against anxiety. We will see in this chapter that waiting is not just sitting around fretfully or impatiently but it is waiting for *the Lord*. We are actually told that we must *choose* waiting. This is an imperative, a command to action. Yes, waiting is action. The implication is firstly that it is good to choose to wait upon the Lord, and secondly, it is implied that one could do otherwise in some cases. For these reasons, we are being commanded here to wait for the Lord. There are times when circumstances require us to take logical steps forward and do something, but what we are describing here are the times when it is best to choose to wait. So what does it mean to wait upon the Lord? That is the first of three questions we will ask ourselves in studying this strategy: What does it mean to be waiting upon the Lord? What do I do while I'm waiting? (How do I wait?) And what benefits come from waiting on the Lord?

What Does It Mean To Be Waiting Upon The Lord?

According to the best Hebrew lexicon, the Hebrew verb *qavah*, which is the term that is translated most frequently in the Old Testament as "to wait," means "to hope for". Hope is not a separate strategy but is tied into waiting. The word means *to hope for*, *to wait for*, or *to look forward with confidence to* that which is good and beneficial. It often includes a real sense of anticipation, the "leaning over your seat" kind of eagerness. We all know what that is like. We can feel this way when we are standing on tiptoe peering over the crowd expectantly for the sight of someone whom we miss dearly because they have been gone a long time, or when we are checking our watches frequently for an important phone call at a specific hour. We can pace or bounce and feel like we are on the edge of our seat. The word itself implies this confident anticipation.

Waiting when we have no control

As Christians, what are we eagerly anticipating? We are anticipating the Lord. About twenty-eight times in the Old Testament, depending on the translation used, the object of the verb, "to wait," is the Lord. Genesis 49:18 says, "I wait for your salvation, Oh Lord." And Lamentations 3:25 states, "The Lord is good to those who wait for him," to those who wait upon the Lord with this confident anticipation. In the life of David, the focus of his and Israel's waiting was for God's providential care as an agrarian culture. They plowed, planted, and pruned, and then they had to wait for the rain and for the harvest. They couldn't control those things, and neither can we today. Consequently, waiting upon the Lord in the Old Testament was predominantly waiting for God's providential care in the seasons of life, like the harvest, and waiting for God's deliverance of their bodies from illnesses that at the time, they had no cures for. They waited for him as well in the salvation of their nation from slavery to other pagan nations, and for the coming of Messiah. Some of these things took many years and many generations of God's people. Their waiting compiled a blending of similarities and differences to our waiting today.

However, when we come to the New Testament, the Greek terms for "waiting" are close in meaning, but the focus is different. In the New Testament, it is not so much a waiting upon God's providential care, though that is obviously true (we still need rain and food and safe shelter), but rather, it is primarily a waiting upon Christ to return, and for the next age to come. It is a waiting for the new heavens and new earth, the Kingdom of God in its fulness. Paul in Philippians 3:20 says, "…our citizenship is in heaven, and from it we await a Savior, the Lord Jesus Christ." Again, he says in Galatians 5:5, "…we ourselves eagerly wait for the hope of righteousness." Looking, then, at the use of the words in both the Old and New Testaments, we can define waiting upon the Lord to mean **trusting confidently that God will act in his time.**

This is not a panicking, fretful, despairing-over-projected-outcomes sort of waiting, but relying upon God's wisdom, his understanding of the situation, and battling to believe that his understanding is better than our understanding. It is a forward-looking hope in God's word. Psalm 130:5 says, "I wait for the Lord, my soul waits, and in his word I hope…" We see again, *hope* as being embedded in waiting. *Hoping* is the confident element of anticipation. We are hoping in his word as we wait. Psalm 130 goes on to say, "…my soul waits for the Lord more than watchmen for the morning, more than watchmen for the morning." The watchmen were the assigned men to stand on the towers or the outer walls that protected the stone city, and they had different shifts, some of which were in the middle of the night. That lone sentry had to vigilantly stand at attention all night and he would be anxious for morning to finally dawn in the east. David is saying that he also waits for the Lord with that sense of hopeful expectancy more than a watchman does for the morning. We have situations like that sometimes; we have to wait for something that is certain, but about which we can do nothing to affect its arrival. Every night the watchman knew morning was going to come, but he could do nothing to make it come any faster. David says, "I wait for the Lord. I have a desire in my soul for God to act, and I have a sense of anticipation that is even greater than that of the night watchmen," and sometimes it is like that for us. We just have to wait for God to work and act, showing us what his decreed will is for our lives.

Waiting even when we could do something

There is another kind of waiting where we choose to wait though we *could* do something about it, though perhaps not the right thing. So, waiting on the Lord secondly means not taking matters into our own hands when there is the possibility that we could do something wrong. It is setting our resolve *not* to seek bringing about our desired goals by turning to our own schemes rather than waiting on God's timing and his provision. Scripture is filled with examples of people who made this mistake, and life didn't get better for them. Think of Abraham and Sarah. Abraham was the father of the Abrahamic Covenant, the father of the people of God. We are called the children of Abraham, so important was this patriarch. God made that glorious promise to him and Sarah that he would give them a son. Through Sarah, that son would become a distant descendant of the One who would be the source of blessing to all nations, tribes and tongues. But they needed to wait. And they waited…and waited…they waited a decade. Two decades. They waited three decades, then four decades. They waited *five* decades…finally, they got tired of waiting. Sarah said, "Where is this promise?" Then she convinced Abraham to go in to her handmaiden, and Ishmael was born to them. But Ishmael was not God's promised child. And this became a problem for them. This was not God's way of fulfilling the promise; it was a compromise that brought great difficulties into their lives and his descendants down through the centuries.

There was also King Saul who in his impatience couldn't wait for the priest to come and fulfill the priestly activities of worship and sacrifice to the Lord. As king, he said, "I'm tired of waiting…I'll do it." Henceforth, he was rejected as king in Israel because God said that was not the way he wanted things to be done. Saul had known that, but he grew impatient (1 Sam. 13:5-14). There are many situations in our lives where it is clear that it should be done in a certain way, but we must first wait, and we get tired of waiting due to the strain of anxiety. So, we try to bring it about some other way through our own schemes or techniques, our own fleshly strength. But waiting means not taking matters into our own hands, especially when we know it is second best or not morally right.

What Do I Do While I'm Waiting?

Waiting involves resting

So what are we to do while we wait? Or, to state it differently, how do we wait? First of all, as we have said, waiting upon God is not entirely a passive state. It is both active and passive. There is a passive component to waiting, like we saw for the watchman waiting for the morning (he can do what he's doing, which is watching, but he can't do anything to bring about the morning). This is a resting in God's timing, resting in God's decisions for our lives, resting in God's knowledge and understanding. As we rest we take time to remember. Waiting times are times to actively take time to sit down and say, "Lord, help me remember what you've done for me." They are times to be thankful. They are times to ask yourselves, "How has my life changed since I became a believer? What has God done?" Waiting time is a time to rehearse the past like David did. He says he is confident, because he has seen his enemy fall. He had his Goliath and God championed his glory over the Philistine pagan nation and saved David's life. It is a time to go backwards and find fresh strength to continue waiting because you see how trustworthy God has been to you before. It's a time for you to think, as a Christian, about all that God has done for you in the cross of Jesus Christ; to go back and grasp again the basic foundational ideas, such as the fact that he loves you because he gave himself for you while you were yet a rebel. These are times to go over the situations in your life that he has blessed, and the things he has done for you.

Indeed, having seen Psalm 27 in its entirety, we may conclude that David, before affirming he will wait upon the Lord, has been practicing all the other spiritual activities we noted to this point: *trusting* by reflecting on what God has done for him, *seeking* his face and protective love, *asking* him for his presence and deliverance, and *following* God in obedience. Consider now how they are each woven together into his walk with the Lord and conspire to strengthen his heart.

Waiting involves trusting

Waiting involves trusting God's timing and his sovereign authority; it is trusting that God rules over all the situations and the details of your life. God rules over the nations and over circumstances. Therefore, when you are trusting his timing, you are trusting his majesty, his sovereignty, his control, and his authority. Scripture says, "Our God is in the heavens, he does whatever he pleases" (Psalm 115:3 NASB). He can fix or fulfill whatever you are facing in an instant, should he so choose. And sometimes he chooses to act swiftly, while at other times, it appears that he delays. Yet all events are completed in our lives and in the world according to the perfect will and timing of the One who has planned it all. God is never early nor does he arrive late. He acts precisely when and how he has decreed he will, and our role as his trusting children is to wait for his sovereign providence, for we know it is the best thing for us. Psalm 37:7 says, "Be still before the Lord and wait patiently for him; fret not yourself over the one who prospers in his way, over the man who carries out evil devices!" Sometimes we might be tempted to think, "Look at those people getting rich! Life's going better for them. He's a liar and a jerk yet look how much money he makes!" Fret not, God says, and do not act rashly. "Refrain from anger, and forsake wrath. Fret not yourself, for it tends only to evil. For the evildoers shall be cut off" (Psalm 37:8-9). Take a long look at the brevity of your life and lift your eyes to the eternal promises held out for us in Christ which never perish. Those who wait for the Lord shall one day inherit the land. It is just a matter of time. The kingdom is coming in just a little while. The wicked will be no more. And though you look carefully at his place, he will not be there. Wait, wait for God. What is it to wait upon the Lord? It is to trust confidently and expectantly that God will act. It means to not take matters into your own hands when you know it is wrong. It's not the best, it's second best at best. Trust his sovereignty. He is in control. He can change your life in just a minute, should he choose to.

Waiting involves seeking

Waiting time is also a time to seek. Remember verse 4 of our psalm: "This one thing I shall seek, to dwell in the house of the Lord forever." Waiting is a time to restore personal intimacy with God if you have lost it. Ask yourself, "Is Christ the center of my life? Do I cherish my relationship with God above all else?" Perhaps you are afraid because you have made something else more important which is now being threatened. Remind yourself that everything in this life is going to fade away except him. This is the time to evaluate your motives and ask, "What are the priorities of my life? Lord, teach me. Why is this thing that I'm waiting for so important to me? Why am I so fearful about this thing? Has this pushed God to the side? Should it be this important? Teach me, Lord, and lead me." As we seek him to show us where our heart's allegiance lies, we will find that the ability to wait is granted to us because the weight of anticipation of our desired outcome shifts to a fully satisfied, restful contentment in him. Andrew Murray shares,

> *God's eye is upon his people; their eye is upon Him. In waiting upon God, our eye, looking up to him, meets his looking down upon us. This is the blessedness of waiting upon God, that it takes our eyes and thoughts away from ourselves, even our needs and desires, and occupies us with our God.*[39]

Our needs can become a source of worry, but as we fix our eye upon him as Murray states, we will find the wait more

---

[39] Andrew Murray, *Waiting on God*, (Chicago ILL: Moody Press, 1961), 54.

bearable for he will firstly bear it with us, comforting us, but also because the urgency of the need or desire begins to dull in the light of his presence and relationship with us.

So, waiting is time to seek for the one thing again, to refresh that deepening of our relationship with Christ. We wait with eagerness for him, and when we wait for him above all other "waits", we will find peace in him. Also remember that you will be rewarded in seeking him. Remember Jeremiah who said on behalf of the Lord, "You will seek me and you will find me when you seek me with all your heart" (Jer. 29:13). I know that there are times when we won't seek God with all our heart until he puts us in a situation where we have to wait, and after going through that, we realize that God has been drawing us to remove our eyes from the dreaded (or happy) anticipation of something temporal, and onto a longing expectation of him each day. Like Adam and Eve in the garden of Eden, before sin came into the world, their highest anticipation I believe was to meet with him and enjoy his comforting, steady, overflowing love and companionship. To speak to him of their day and what they saw and did. Or what they desired to do with him tomorrow. When we find ourselves patiently and quietly waiting, like a child happy to hum and sit on the ground, busying himself with his play for he knows his mother is near, we will suddenly see him act or hear him finally say, "Now is the time," and then we will marvel. We will think, "Wow, how capable God is, and how wise! I can see his plan was best, and his timing was perfect."

Waiting involves asking

In Psalm 27:7, we saw David cry out in prayer, and that is a third practice for us to do while we are waiting. We pray. Waiting is a time to knock on the door, and to keep seeking to learn to persevere in prayer. When we wait, we ought to repeatedly turn to God and keep speaking to God about the things that we are waiting for, that thing which is really burdening us, that which is causing anxiety in our lives. This might be as frequently as twenty, thirty, forty times a day when our hearts are overflowing with nervous distress and racing thoughts. Pause and pray for peace, wisdom and for discernment. James 1 tells us that if we lack wisdom during a trial, we only need to ask God for it. The Lord is not stingy with his counsel, and he delights in showing us his ways. As we mature in Christ, we will learn to pray when we have to wait for God to act in our lives. We learn dependence because, like the watchman, we cannot make the morning come any sooner. The night of prayerful watching teaches us dependence upon God. Remember Christ's practical reasoning that to worry and fret in this life does no good, for it cannot add a single day to our life, nor change the impossible that only God can change. Jesus shared this truth with us knowing that this reminder will help train our minds to think rationally (as in to think within reality, dwelling upon a truthful fact he has declared/created) when our emotions lead us from trusting in him. His sovereign rule and plan over our lives can give us even physical healing and restoration, for when we are consumed with worry and fear, the stress within our bodies and souls can take quite a toll. Remember Psalm 4:8 that gives a picture of the psalmist able to restfully enjoy the gift of sleep for he has entrusted all that has occurred that day (and what may occur tomorrow), into the hands of his loving God: "In peace I will both lie down and sleep, for you alone, O Lord, make me dwell in safety" (Psalm 4:8).

The physical and the spiritual are truly knitted together, especially in times of waiting, I believe. Sleep, for many, escapes them during times of anxiety, and I recall a time when a lack of sleep added greatly to an affliction the Lord had brought to us. My wife Sheri had a spur in her lower spine from a previous injury, and for two years we waited for my wife's health to return. During this time she was often in severe pain and emotional distress, and she could not sit or lie comfortably. Sleeping for both of us was both a physical and spiritual struggle. For nearly one whole year she couldn't sleep in a bed, so every night we would kiss and say, "Goodnight, honey," and she would limp, bent over, to the chair downstairs, and I would try and sleep in the bedroom upstairs, but concern for her and her nightly absence made it difficult to find peace. As this trial dragged on, each day and each night we prayed and prayed. Though we were both tired, we both learned to pray. We both grew in perseverance of prayer, knowing the whole time that our God was in the heavens; he does whatever he pleases. We learned that if Sheri was not healed today, it meant that it didn't please him to heal her now. If another six months passed and she was still not healed, it was not pleasing him to heal her now. It did change after a year, praise God, and we have been thankful for both his answer to prayer and the growth to our faith.

Some of you are in situations like that. Spiritually restless, physically worn, emotionally harassed, wading through a trial in your life. I know that many people and families in our church have their particular difficulties and burdens to bear. I know their trials, and have prayed for them. I encourage you, reader, to persevere in prayer while you are waiting and resting in God's timing, resting in God's sovereignty, resting in God's knowledge. He knows and sees all that is best and good for you, and he desires that for you. If he delays, it is because it is better for you, though it may not seem that way right now. You must believe this, despite how unsure you may feel, because he is your Heavenly Father, and he loves you. He would never do anything wrong for you or anything out of any degree of spite. Sometimes we see through a fog; we see things dimly. We wonder if he could be doing something better for us. But God knows best. You must be convinced of that. You'll never be content until you learn to rest in God's sovereignty and his knowledge, and simultaneously believe he loves you. Are you convinced God is almighty and sovereign? Are you convinced God loves you? Then hold onto both of those truths when the timing of your life and the things that are causing you great anxiety do not work out as you have planned or designed. So, pray while you wait.

Waiting involves following

Fourthly, we follow while we wait. David asked the Lord to teach him while he waited. Remember that God's way would be walking in his moral principles. What is the right thing to think and do at this time of my life? Lead me in that way, on that level path. It is not an obstacle-free path, but a path that is true and right. You might feel like saying, "The rules are making me dizzy. Everyone is telling me to do this, or do that, but you tell me to wait. So, what should I do? What should I say? How should I act at this juncture of my life?" This is the time to ask the Lord that question, not just your friends or pastor. Look to him and lay before him your situation, asking him to show you what to do. This could be a time to wait, or a time to act. For example, as you wait for an answer of whether or not you as a family are being called to move, you can wait upon the Lord to show you his answer while also making preparations that would be helpful in the event that you do move. Or you may begin to encourage small conversations with your children about these things, praying as a family, being wise in not removing all ties with friends or sports activities just yet, in the event that you don't move. All these things could be following the Lord's moral will, his path for you, as you wait upon him. We must form the habit of saying in waiting times, "Lord, teach me and lead me." Then, it is a time to follow, a time to obey, a time to make sure you are doing what is right in your life, and take action. All these things that David speaks about in this psalm are the things you can be doing while you wait.

Waiting involves listening

Sometimes we are waiting for God's counsel, which is the specific truth from his word that applies in one's life right now. When you are in this situation, ask yourself, "What is the combination of truths from Scripture that applies to the circumstances I am in? What are the promises in his word that I should be relying upon right now to help me make a decision?" Sometimes the pressures of life make us feel like we must come to a quick resolution. We feel panicky and "unraveled." We want to rush to relieve the anxiety we feel about it. The panting hunt for relief takes over. Stop and wait. Say, "Lord, I am waiting for your counsel. I'm waiting for you to break through my mind with clarity, helping me to see clearly that these are the things I should be thinking, deciding and doing or saying right now." This is waiting for the counsel of the Lord, and not living life by your own perspective, strength or emotions.

Israel often failed to do that, and unfortunately, they paid a price for it. In 1 Corinthians 10:11 Paul explains those failures and consequences were "written down for our instruction" (as in, take heed and learn!). Israel's forty-year wandering in the desert as a consequence for their disbelief and fear was written for your instruction. Their failure in the desert to trust God was written for your benefit. Psalm 106:13 says of them, "But they soon forgot his works; they did not wait for his counsel." And so it is with many a Christian; we do not wait for his counsel. And why is that? Because we forget his works. We forget who Jesus Christ is. We forget that he is the Lord of Glory. We forget that he has the power of the resurrection: "I am the resurrection and the life." We lose sight that he is the one who upholds all things by the word of his power. We neglect all these things about Christ, not only his love, but his nature as truly divine. Having forgotten his works, we fail to wait for his counsel, and we make a decision too soon based on emotion, based on fears, based on self-preservation. Surely, all of us have failed in this way at some point, so, let us **remember** right now, that as Christians, there is forgiveness for every time we fail to wait, because he paid for the sin of our impatience or foolishness just as well as every other sin. We can thank him for that and seek his help to remember all his works—this is the key to a trusting, patient heart while waiting for his counsel.

Waiting involves self-counsel

In verse 13, David shifts the language of his prayer and preaches to himself. MacLaren remarks, "The heart that spoke to God now speaks to itself."[40] There are several details to highlight. First of all, the verb in this verse is now first person singular. He says, "*I* believe *I* shall look upon the goodness of the Lord in the land of the living.*"* There is in some Hebrew texts a word in this sentence that is sometimes omitted in modern translations. The New American Standard and others include it and translate it as "unless." When included, the sentence would read something like this: "I would have despaired *unless* I believed that I would see the goodness of the Lord in the land of the living." The ESV decides to set that phrase aside because it is difficult to be sure about the translation, but I believe the New American Standard and others are correct to include it in the verse. There is a sense here that David is now talking to himself. He is doing what he does in so many psalms; he preaches to himself: "I would have despaired unless I believed that I would see the goodness of the Lord in the land of living." And truly he *has* seen the goodness of God! He has seen foes fall before him time and again because God delivered him. Therefore, he says to himself and to us, "Wait for the Lord." David is preaching the gospel, as it were, to himself again, reminding himself to wait and trust. David's faith in God's

---

[40] *MacLaren*, 267.

future deliverance and grace to him is strongly rooted in his experience of God's help and answered prayers in the present life he was living. If he could not see this goodness of God to him in his life today, how could he believe in God's goodness to come for tomorrow? For the next day? For the next ten years? And for his eternal soul? We need to testify like David, that God's goodness can and *IS* seen today in our lives, and let this truth affirm our faith in him to provide for tomorrow. This reflection redeems our times of waiting tenfold. Instead of dwelling over and over on the difficulties in our lives, we can proclaim to our own souls God's faithfulness and "take heart." God has overcome, and he will overcome once more in the particular circumstance you are in. David says, "Be strong and let your heart take courage. Wait for the Lord, because, if I had not believed that I would see the goodness of God in this land and not just in eternity to come, I would have despaired." Wait and let the best come to you. Trust in his timing and his sovereignty. This is purposeful action.

Many people determinedly tell themselves things, but they are the wrong things. They look in the mirror, and say to themselves, "Oh, you loser!" They should go the next step to say, "Oh, you loved-by-Christ loser. Oh, you loser for whom Christ died and gave his life and loves!" Don't delude yourself thinking you are either too sinful to save or to change, or too righteous to need saving. Don't wallow in self-talk that only creates a more self-absorbed, distorted view of yourself. Preach to yourself the gospel, the good news. Convince yourself of God's goodness as you've seen in the gospel because you believe in Christ. Preach to the person in the mirror the truth of the gospel. Paul had a way of doing that in the New Testament. He would use the word that is translated in English, "I reckon," or "I consider," especially in the book of Romans, to preach to himself. For example, Romans 8:18 states, "I consider that the sufferings of this present time are not worth comparing with the glory that is to be revealed to us." Paul is saying, "I've come to a settled conviction about this and I tell myself this again and again." Paul is preaching the promise of the resurrection to Paul! I can picture him in a dungeon. He's beat up. His back is scarred. He's a prisoner chained to the wall, and he tells himself that the sufferings of this present world are not even worthy to be compared with the glories that are going to be revealed to him. I can imagine Paul preaching to himself like this over and over until the Roman guard chained to him tells him to be quiet. I can hear him preach the gospel not just to others, but to himself. And David is doing this in Psalm 27 as he comes to the end. This is self-exhortation.

Over the years of my ministry, many individuals waiting and evaluating a decision have said to me, "I've decided to listen to my heart." At that point, *my* heart goes, "Arrgh!" I am deeply concerned for them because Scripture says our hearts are exceedingly deceitful. Most of the time we must not listen to our hearts but preach to them. Do not let your heart speak to you about what it desires; *inform* your heart what the Scriptures says it *should* desire. What in Christ it *can* desire. Take the truth that God is saying and let that light shine upon it because your heart will say lesser things. It will whisper, "It's not worth it." It will demand, "Enough is enough. Where's God? Let's move on." When we hear things like that from our hearts, let's do ourselves a favor and don't listen to them! Exhort yourself, daily saturating yourself with the living waters of the gospel in Christ, for from your heart "flow the springs of life" (Prov. 4:23). Whatever we pour into our souls is what will come gushing out, and we want life-giving streams of thought when trials bear down upon us. When our hearts flood full of Christ, we shall be able to wait with steadfastness and courage: "Blessed is the man who trusts in the Lord, whose trust is the Lord. He is like a tree planted by water, that sends out its roots by the stream, and does not fear when heat comes, for its leaves remain green, and is not anxious in the year of drought, for it does not cease to bear fruit" (paraphrasing Psalm 1).

The Benefits of Waiting

We must recognize that if our Lord makes us wait, it must be purposeful, because God doesn't make mistakes. And because he is our Heavenly Father, it is also loving. I cannot stress it enough that we must be convinced of this. This is something we must repeat to ourselves every day--that God is true. He's right. He's just. He's perfect and he loves us. He is sovereign. If we are waiting, it is not that God forgot to do something. It is because he has planned it.

What comes to those who wait is the blessing of God, which in this life means *growth* more than anything else. What comes is change...the transforming power to reorient our life around God, so that whatever has been making us tearful and upset now may not produce that same response again next year because we have experienced maturing. We are surely overcoming, for God has overcome all sin that hinders us from arriving safely home with him. Through Christ's victory, be assured, something is happening while you wait. God is bringing forth fruit in your life in the forms of a more loving and pure desire for God, godly character, and good works. Another excerpt from Paul Tripp's blog on Psalm 27 says,

> *Waiting on God isn't to be viewed as an obstruction in the way of the plan. Waiting is an essential part of the plan. For the child of God, waiting isn't simply about what I'll receive at the end of my wait. No, waiting is much more purposeful, efficient, and practical than that. Waiting is fundamentally about what I'll become as I wait. God is using the wait to*

do in and through me exactly what He's promised.
Through the wait He's changing me.[41]

Indeed, you are becoming more and more a reflection of the image of Christ by waiting, because through it, God is refining you into a holy, happy child of God.

Waiting produces endurance

This type of refinement produces endurance. James, the Lord's brother says in essense that, "those who wait upon the Lord are those who are in a time of testing." Testing asks the question, will you be loyal? Will you be faithful to the Lord, or will you choose your own way? For this reason, the test becomes a way of strengthening your faith. That is God's design. James 1:2-3 puts it this way: "Count it all joy, my brothers, when you meet trials of various kinds for you know that the testing of your faith produces steadfastness." This is not the testing of a teacher who wants to make his students fail and so conjures clever questions to fool them, but the kind of testing that a mother bird does when she nudges the little chick out of the nest, testing the wings so they grow stronger. Other translations of James 1 use the term "endurance" in place of "steadfastness," which means the ability to bear up under a heavy weight. If we never were under such heavy weight, we'd never know that God is able to sustain us through them. We may be going through a difficulty to learn that God can sustain us to endure an even bigger one that is coming! James goes on to say, in verse 4, "And let steadfastness have its full effect, that you may be perfect and complete, lacking in nothing." This journey of perfection in godliness could be summed up in our one word "endurance". Indeed, to be "perfect and complete" will only come through times that require it. Endurance is an essential

---

[41] Paul Tripp, "Psalm 27: Productive Delay," Paul Tripp Ministries, August 20, 2007, http://paultrippministries.blogspot.com/2007/08/psalm-29-productive-delay.html

component of the Christian life. The book of Hebrews is all about that. In fact, towards the end in Hebrews 10:36, the writer says, "For you have need of endurance, so that when you have done the will of God you may receive what is promised." If you are going to receive the blessings of the kingdom to come, you must endure. I shake my head now as I write this, for we have great need of learning it, but it is not the lesson we like, is it? (We would like patience, but we want it right now!) But this only comes through the stretching of those faith muscles, learning to wait, and embracing the fact that we cannot make a short-cut around it. God has placed us all in individual situations that require the wait, for only then will we grow in endurance.

Waiting produces courage

Waiting also produces courage. Returning to Psalm 27, David says, "Wait for the Lord; be strong, and let your heart take courage; wait for the Lord!" He says "let your heart take courage" as an imperative, but let's consider what he means in the context. He had said, "I would have despaired *unless* I believed that I would see the goodness of God in the land of the living." Then he says "wait for the Lord" twice, with "be strong and let your heart take courage" sandwiched in between these two last commands to wait for the Lord. Those two verbs, *be strong* and let your heart *take courage* or *take heart,* are the same ones used in Joshua to encourage the Israelites as they were about to cross the River Jordan and take the Promised Land. They were about to face fierce battle. Interestingly, those two verbs are coupled together in this manner 12 times in the Old Testament.[42] "Be strong. Take heart." They are often used together to encourage the people of God right before they are about to face something extremely difficult or some task that appears seemingly

---

[42] See Deut. 31:6, 7, 23; Joshua 1:6, 7, 9, 18, 10:25; 1 Chron. 22:13, 28:20; 2 Chron. 32:7; Psa. 31:24.

impossible. David says to himself and to us, the readers, "While you wait, be strong, and take heart."

The imperative, "be strong" is actually in a passive form, as in to *be strengthened*, meaning we are actually *being strengthened* as we wait. How does that happen? It is what *God* is doing during the waiting. He is actively working on us. He is encouraging us. If we are faithfully seeking the Lord, remembering his past faithfulness, prayerfully asking, and telling him to lead us as we follow, God will strengthen us. The more we see him as we wait and study and lean into him, the more courage we are given, because true Christian courage arises from a quiet confidence in knowing the Lord. This is why Paul can say, "when I am weak, then I am strong." The strength is not his. God's strength comes to us in our weakness. Charles Spurgeon said, "...waiting upon the Lord produces the effect of increasing our courage because it often gives us a sight of the eternal reward, and if a man gets a glimpse of the crown of glory, the crown of thorns will no more prick his temples."[43] So it is in the weakness of waiting, those thorny seasons of knowing that we cannot do this alone and that we cannot bring it about, that we will be strengthened and gain courage. Seek the Lord and sit at his feet, gazing at his beauty, for "they who wait for the Lord shall renew their strength. They shall mount up with wings like eagles" (Isa. 40:31).

If you have ever seen eagles fly, you may have noticed that they don't do a lot of flapping. Eagles fly higher than any other species of bird, yet they are carried up by the wind. When you think of this verse, "they shall mount up with wings," don't think of that huge albatross on the beach, huffing and puffing, or the pelican trying desperately to get

---

[43] Charles Spurgeon, "Brave Waiting," The Spurgeon Center for Biblical Preaching at Midwestern Seminary, accessed March 18, 2020, https://www.spurgeon.org/resource-library/sermons/brave-waiting/#flipbook/

up in the air. Rather, imagine: the whistling wind barrels and rolls across the sky, swooping up an eagle when the eagle has just positioned himself in the right way. Even somebody like David, living centuries before us in Palestine, would know this because he had seen plenty of eagles soar, and most of the time it would appear so effortless. The wind just took them up, right off the cliffs. This, then, is the experience of those who wait on the Lord, that in the weakest times of life, a time of heavy anxiety, a moment will come when we will rise up with wings like an eagle… "we shall run and not be weary. We shall walk and not faint." Look up to his face with full heart and you will feel him carry you up. Thus, we grow in courage while we wait upon the Lord. I think it is worth noting what Alexander Maclaren commented on this verse saying, "None but those who wait on the Lord will be at once conscious of weakness and filled with strength, aware of the foes and bold to meet them."[44] Thus, with Paul we proclaim, "when I am weak, then I am strong" (2 Cor. 12:10).

Waiting produces hope

As we wait upon the Lord, we grow not only in our endurance, our courage and our strength, but we grow in hope. Waiting involves hoping. We noted already that it is part of the meaning of the word *to wait*. It is embedded in Psalm 62:5: "For God alone, O my soul, wait in silence, for my hope is from him." Waiting builds our hope because hope is that sense of assurance that what God has promised about the future is going to be true. While we are waiting upon God and seeking him, seeing an answer to prayer right here in the land of the living, our hope is growing. Our sense of confidence that God is true, the gospel is real, and there is a resurrection unto an unimaginably glorious future grows stronger. "Yes!" our hearts cry out. "There is a new creation

---

[44] *MacLaren*, 267.

coming!" That is Christian hope. This hope rises as we wait.

Waiting produces all this and so much more. Waiting is not a wrong turn in God's plan for our lives. It is not an obstacle to our sanctification in the Christian life. It is an essential agent of it. Life isn't about what we are "going to get" at the end of waiting, like a child who behaved well solely for the satisfaction of getting a chocolate bar at the end of the program. We may never get that chocolate bar, or that vacation at the beach, or that freedom from a disease or financial distress. God's answer may be "no" to these desires. God hasn't promised all the things in this life. He will show his goodness here in the land of the living, but he will not answer every single prayer you have in the land of living with a "yes." This can be difficult to believe when your life feels like it is going nowhere, or in a painful, unpleasant direction.

Nevertheless, there is coming a day when every promise of God will be fulfilled, ultimately, when he returns for us. On that day, the Scriptures affirm, "And after you have suffered a little while, the God of all grace, who has called you to his eternal glory in Christ, will himself restore, confirm, strengthen, and establish you" (1 Pet. 5:10). Even that thief cancer which robs a loved one of life, or your own life, God himself will destroy and restore you in a new, glorified body. Even that relationship in your life which never heals, but always causes fresh emotional pain, God will finally one day bring everlasting peace to you. Every distress, every fear, every difficulty God will "make up for" and so much more, in the age to come with him. Whatever is lacking here as a result of sin, God will ultimately correct, bring to rights, and make anew. We will have *him*, and we will be perfectly, overflowingly satisfied. David's heart was full of hope, partly because he had seen God fulfill many things in his life, and he rehearsed those things as he waited. He waited until he was strengthened, and he was filled with that hope in his heart. Waiting produces this as we focus our attention on the Lord and the future, and all that he has promised. Our Lord, the greater David, knew this better than all. Thus, he endured the sufferings of the cross "for the joy set before him" (Heb. 12:2).

Choosing To Wait

"The Pilgrim's Progress" is an allegory of the Christian life written by the Puritan John Bunyan, and it is one of the best-loved and most widely read books in English literature. It has been so popular that it has been continuously in print from its first publication to the present day. It traces the journey of one man called Christian from the moment he was converted to the moment he arrives at the Celestial City, heaven. There are many stops along the way. One stop is the Interpreter's house where various scenes take place that are all meant to teach a spiritual lesson. The scene I want to draw your attention to is the scene where two children are sitting on chairs. One child is named Patience and the other child's name is Passion. Bunyan descriptively writes,

> *"I saw in my dream that the Interpreter again took Christian by the hand, and he led him into a very small room in which there sat two little children each on his chair. The name of the elder was Passion and the name of the other was Patience. Passion seemed to be very discontented, while Patience remained calm and quiet. And then Christian asked, 'What is the reason for Passion's unrest?' And the Interpreter replied, 'The Governor of these children would have him wait for the best things that are to be bestowed at the beginning of the next year, but he wants to have his inheritance now, while Patience is quite willing to wait.' And then I saw a person come to Passion and bring him a bag of Treasure that was immediately poured out at his feet. At this, the older child rejoiced, and at the same time he scornfully laughed at Patience. However, I noticed that very soon Passion's wealth*

wasted away with the result that he found himself left with nothing but rags.

And Christian said, 'Explain this matter to me.' And Interpreter said, 'These two lads are symbols (portrayals) of the men of this world; Patience represents those people who are prepared to wait for that which is to come. On the other hand, you will notice that Passion must have all his inheritance now, this very year, that is, in this present world. And so are the people of this world. They insist on having all their good things now, and they cannot possibly wait till next year, that is, the world to come, for lasting treasure. And so that proverb, 'A bird in the hand is worth two in the bush,' that proverb is of more authority with them than of all the divine promises, all the divine testimonies of the good things promised in the world to come. But, as you saw, Passion quickly wasted away all that he had, so he ended up having nothing but rags. And so it will be for all like people at the end of this age. And Christian said, 'Well, now I see that Patience has superior wisdom, and that for several reasons; one, because he's willing to wait for the best things, and also because the glory of his inheritance will last when that of Passion has long ago been reduced to rags.' And then Interpreter said, 'Yes, and we may add another reason. It is that the glory of the next world will never wear out, while the glory of the present decays and then is suddenly gone.'"[45]

Let us also exercise this superior wisdom and trust the promises of God. Keep waiting and stay faithful; don't take matters into your own hands. You will be mocked in this world because you are surrounded by Passions and not by

---

[45] John Bunyan, *The Pilgrim's Progress,* (Wheaton: ILL, Tyndale House, 1991), 28-29.

Patience. You are surrounded by those who love the world, that which is so fleeting and gone in a moment, and not by those who love the world to come. When you say that you are choosing to say "no" to a marital relationship because the person you know is not a believer, yet you are one, know that as you honor the Lord and you continue to wait as a single believer, and your life starts going by, you will be mocked. Young person, when you say "no" to premarital sex because you want to save yourself for the beauty of the intimacy with a spouse, within the context of a covenant that is safe with the promise of faithfulness, you will be mocked, because you are surrounded with people of passion, who want it all now in this world. And when you say "no" to a new job, even though you will make better money, because you know that saying yes to this job is going to involve compromise, you will be mocked because you are surrounded by people of passion and not people of patience. And sometimes God will say "no", and this life will end without him ever saying "yes."

Yet I can say to you today, the Lord is good to all those who wait upon him, and he has always done good things in your life, and that choice must have been the best choice, because it was *his* choice, and only God knows how it was better than what you were hoping for in this life. Right now, in this moment there are Christians all over this globe for whom God is saying "no" to things that you and I take almost as a daily right. These other believers are bearing up faithfully while God is saying "no" to things like an abundance of food every day sitting in the refrigerator. He's saying "no" to the freedom of worshipping Christ in public. "No" to having a family of children. "No" to a life without fear of someone coming and breaking in. 2020 was the year of Covid-19 in which God said "no" in so many ways to so many people. But the truth is, there are Christians all over the globe who consistently live like that. Every believer waits for the answers of prayer dearest to their hearts. Can you wait? Can you stay faithful in this culture? O my friends, trust that what God will bring will be better. Believe him. Believe his promises to you. Wait upon the Lord and with the light of his promises before you, your anxieties will steadily dissipate like a mist and you will be lifted up by his grace.

Whom Shall I Fear?

EPILOGUE

"The beginning of anxiety is the end of faith, and the beginning of true faith is the end of anxiety."[46]

Allow me to say again that fears and anxieties are normal human experiences in a sin broken world. The goal is not to never fear or experience anxiety, for some anxiety is but a necessary warning alarm that something is wrong and needs to be addressed. The goal is to learn how to respond to our fears and anxieties so as to successfully navigate through these God-ordained turbulent waters in ways that bring honor and glory to God and bring us deeper and closer to our Lord, both in our understanding of him and our becoming like him (2 Cor. 3:18). The goal is to learn to battle against unbelief and this will bring us an increasing measure of peace in the midst of anxiety producing circumstances.

---

[46] George Mueller is often attributed with a version of this saying, and the quote (with attribution to Mueller) appears as early as 1897 in The Churchman. However, no source written by Mueller can be found to confirm him as having said this.

This book has been an exploration of and expansion upon David's strategy for facing fears and anxieties as expressed in Psalm 27. It is a strategy of faith. As noted early on, the battle against anxiety is at its core a struggle *against* unbelief and *for* faith. This strategy of faith, I have attempted to sum up as consisting of five components or spiritual activities that are both grace-given privileges and personal disciplines carried out by faith in Christ by the power of the Holy Spirit. They are not sequential steps on a ladder of achievement. They are not meritorious acts of obedience that earn God's love. They are Spirit-empowered capacities given to God's children whereby we may experience his peace in the storm. They are God's medicine for anxiety-stricken hearts. I will now, in brief compass, once again pull together and restate these five strands as a parting encouragement.

Trusting – when anxieties press upon you, trust God's protective love as experienced in the past. Remember that in Christ, God has been and remains your light, salvation and stronghold. Reflect especially upon his protective love displayed at the cross where he conquered your greatest enemy. If God is for you this much, who can be against you? (Rom. 8:31). Fight unbelief with gospel truth!

Seeking – when anxieties press upon you, seek the ONE thing above all others to seek—the one thing necessary—an abiding consciousness of God's presence. Communion with God. That "habitual sight of him." How? by gazing at the beauty of the Lord as revealed in Christ. Meditate again and again upon the glorious attributes of the living God as revealed in his word, which attributes are most clearly and fully on display in Jesus. Remember, when you seek him with all your heart, you will find him. This he has promised you. He wants to be known and is ready to draw near to those who draw near to him.

Asking – when anxieties press upon you, pour your heart and soul out to God in prayer and supplication. He loves to hear from you. Ask him for the grace, strength and hope you need and do so with earnest impudence, responsive immediacy, and above all with a childlike familial confidence. He is your loving Father. When you do, "the peace of God will guard your hearts and your minds in Christ Jesus" (Phil. 4:7).

Following – when anxieties press upon you, it's time to follow him as he leads you in his ways. It's a time to learn—perhaps even a time for change? This involves a teachable spirit and a submissive heart, rooted in the fear of the Lord. Remember "the friendship of the Lord is for those who fear him." He is ready to provide insight and guidance. Are you ready to follow where he leads?

Waiting – when anxieties press upon you, don't react impulsively, rather wait upon God's wisdom to break through, wait for God's guidance to become clear, and wait for his strength to renew you. Though it's often a time to act, it's not a time to take matters into your own hands. Remember, waiting is not an obstacle to what God is doing in your life. The objective as you wait is not what you will receive at the end of waiting, but what you are becoming as you wait. You may feel like nothing is happening, but God is always at work in you. Hope is being nourished. Remember, those who wait upon the Lord "will renew their strength."

Whom Shall I Fear?

ABOUT THE AUTHOR

Tony Sanelli is the founding pastor-teacher of Grace Bible Church of Pleasant Hill, CA. He is a graduate of the Master's Seminary and the Southern Baptist Theological Seminary. In conjunction with his ministry at Grace Bible Church, he teaches theology at the Cornerstone Bible College and Seminary, serves on the board and speaks at various nearby and international conferences and camps. He is also the author of *Recovering the Biblical Gospel.*